Mac Basics
Mac OS X Lion Edition

in Simple steps

Thomas Myer

Use your computer with confidence

Get to grips with practical computing tasks with minimal time, fuss and bother.

In Simple Steps guides guarantee immediate results. They tell you everything you need to know on a specific application; from the most essential tasks to master, to every activity you'll want to accomplish, through to solving the most common problems you'll encounter.

Helpful features

To build your confidence and help you to get the most out of your computer, practical hints, tips and shortcuts feature on every page:

 ALERT: Explains and provides practical solutions to the most commonly encountered problems

 HOT TIP: Time and effort saving shortcuts

 SEE ALSO: Points you to other related tasks and information

 DID YOU KNOW? Additional features to explore

WHAT DOES THIS MEAN?
Jargon and technical terms explained in plain English

Practical. Simple. Fast.

Mac Basics
Mac OS X Lion Edition

\

R⌐
by in⁺
in pe
by ph⌐

Prentice Hall
is an imprint of

Harlow, England • London • New York • Boston • San Francisco • Toronto • Sydney • Singapore • Hong Kong
Tokyo • Seoul • Taipei • New Delhi • Cape Town • Madrid • Mexico City • Amsterdam • Munich • Paris • Milan

PEARSON EDUCATION LIMITED

Edinburgh Gate
Harlow CM20 2JE
Tel: +44 (0)1279 623623
Fax: +44 (0)1279 431059
Website: www.pearson.com/uk

First published in Great Britain in 2010
Mac OS X Lion edition 2012

© Thomas Myer 2010, 2012

The right of Thomas Myer to be identified as author of this work has been asserted by him in accordance with the Copyright, Designs and Patents Act 1988.

Pearson Education is not responsible for the content of third-party internet sites.

ISBN: 978-0-273-74636-2

British Library Cataloguing-in-Publication Data
A catalogue record for this book is available from the British Library.

Library of Congress Cataloging-in-Publication Data
A catalog record for this book is available from the Library of Congress.

10 9 8 7 6 5 4 3 2 1
15 14 13 12 11

Image from Google maps on p. 148 © Google Inc.

Designed by pentacorbig, High Wycombe
Typeset in 11/14 pt ITC Stone Sans by 3
Printed in Great Britain by Scotprint, Haddington.

Dedication:

To my wife Hope, for loving me anyway.

Author's acknowledgements:

A book like this never sees the light of day without lots of help, namely:

Neil Salkind, my agent, for bringing this wonderful series to my attention and suggesting that I might be able to add a book to it.

Katy Robinson and Steve Temblett at Pearson UK for putting up with and fielding questions across the pond at near relativistic speeds.

Emma Devlin, Sarah Wild and the production gang over at Pearson UK for working through my grammatical shortcomings – my thanks for shaping all that rough prose into something palatable.

Finally, to my family (divine spouse Hope, two dogs Kafka and Marlowe) for putting up with me being away while writing this book.

Contents at a glance

Contents

Top 10 Mac Tips

1 Getting started with your new Mac

3 Email

4 Web

5 Contacts and events

6 Photos

7 Music

8 Movies

10 Customising your Mac

Top 10 Mac Problems Solved

Top 10 Mac Tips

Introduction

Before we get down to the nitty-gritty of using your Mac, I thought I'd share with you 10 of the coolest things you'll be able to do with it now that you own one. Over time you might develop your own list of 'Top 10 Coolest Things' but each of these here is designed to get you really excited about owning the best personal computing platform in the world.

Tip 1: Take a screenshot

Taking screenshots of whatever is on your Mac screen is a valuable way to keep records of things you see. For example, you might find yourself trying to explain to an IT support person why something just isn't working, then send them a screenshot of what you see.

Your Mac comes with a very good screenshot utility with a number of built-in keyboard shortcuts:

- Pressing ⌘ Shift 3 will take a screenshot of the entire screen and save the results to the Desktop as a file.
- Pressing ⌘ Shift 4, then selecting an area with your mouse, will take a screenshot of an area and save it to the Desktop as a file.
- Pressing ⌘ Control Shift 3 will take a screenshot of the whole screen, then save the image to the clipboard. You can then paste that image wherever you need to.
- Pressing ⌘ Control Shift 4, then selecting an area with your mouse, will take a screenshot of that area and save the image to the clipboard.
- Pressing ⌘ Control Shift 4, then pressing space and clicking a window, will take a screenshot of that window and save the image to the clipboard.

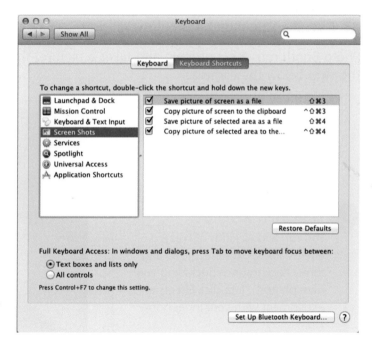

Tip 2: Take a photo of yourself

What could be more fun than taking a self-portrait? Imagine the fun you could have if you could do that – you could do some serious shots, some goofy ones, even include friends and family in the shots.

Well, thankfully, your Mac comes with a neat application called Photo Booth. It's precisely like those photo booths you see at carnivals, except without curtains and bubble gum under the cushions.

To take a photo of yourself:

1 Open Photo Booth by opening the Finder, clicking on Applications and double-clicking Photo Booth.

2 Pose yourself, adjusting yourself with the help of the preview screen.

3 Click the Snapshot button (it's white with a black camera icon on it).

Photo Booth runs a countdown and takes a picture. You'll see your image show up in the strip below the camera.

? DID YOU KNOW?

You can add all kinds of crazy effects, like sepia tone, glows and funny backgrounds (including your own photos!). Just click Effects and experiment with your inner goofy kid.

3

Tip 3: Switch between applications and documents quickly

If you're even remotely busy, you'll probably have all kinds of applications and documents open. It's easy to tell which applications are open by looking at the Dock icons (any open applications will have a little light on under them, like somebody is home) but sometimes that's not enough.

- If you want to see all your open windows at once, press F9.
- If you just want to see all the windows of the current application, press F10.
- If you want to see the Desktop, press F11. This will move all the open windows off to the side.
- You can use ⌘ Tab to cycle through all your different applications one at a time.
- You can also use ⌘ ~ to cycle through one application's windows or documents. This is an excellent way to see all the emails you've got open, for example.

Tip 4: Change your Desktop background picture

As lovely as your default Mac Desktop background is, you probably don't want to keep it around for ever, right? Well, it's pretty easy to change it.

To change your Desktop background:

1 Select System Preferences from the Apple menu.

2 Click Desktop & Screen Saver.

3 Click Desktop at the top of the screen.

4 Choose one of the Apple image categories, an iPhoto library or a folder from your Mac.

5 Click one of the images from that group.

6 Close System Preferences by clicking the red button in the upper left corner of the window.

? DID YOU KNOW?

You can also get to this screen by control-clicking the Desktop and choosing Change Desktop Background from the pop-up menu.

Tip 5: Using Launchpad

If you're an iPad user and love the way you can easily access iPad apps, then you're going to love Launchpad on Mac OS X Lion. Basically, Launchpad displays all your applications in the same style as the iPad. You can organise your applications into folders, too!

To access Launchpad:

1 Click the Launchpad button on your Dock. It looks like a rocket ship.

2 Simply click an application's icon to launch it.

1

? DID YOU KNOW?

You can create folders by dragging one icon onto another. So, you might create a folder with favourite utilities by dragging iCal onto the Address Book.

Tip 6: Set up smart mailboxes in Mail

A smart mailbox is a very powerful idea: instead of having static mailboxes with manually placed email in them, how about a smart mailbox that looks out for whatever email you tell it to watch for? Imagine being able to quickly find:

- All emails with a certain subject line.
- All emails from a certain group of people.
- All emails you received last week that were marked important.
- All emails you received last week with attachments.
- All emails you sent to a certain person.

A smart mailbox will find emails that match its search criteria no matter where they actually live in Mail. This makes it an ideal solution for those who like to tuck their emails into a whole bunch of nested folders but still need ready access to them.

To create a smart mailbox, do one of the following:

- Click the + button at the bottom of the sidebar and choose New Smart Mailbox from the menu.
- Alternatively, choose Mailbox > New Smart Mailbox from the menu.

 HOT TIP: You can edit a smart mailbox once you've created it. Simply control-click it and choose Edit Smart Mailbox from the menu.

Once you do either of those, give your new smart mailbox an appropriate name and then use the + button to add criteria to your smart mailbox. For example, to always see email you've received in the past three days but haven't replied to:

1 Name the Smart Mailbox 'Last 3 Days Unreplied Mail'.

2 Choose Date Received from the first dropdown.

3 Choose 'is in the last' from the second dropdown.

4 Enter a 3 in the text field.

5 Click the + button.

6 Choose Message was not Replied to in the dropdown.

7 Click OK.

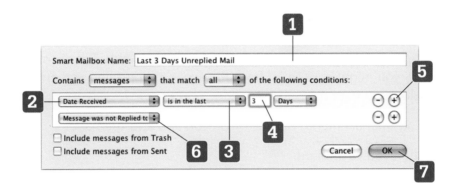

Tip 7: Set up smart playlists in iTunes

If you liked smart mailboxes in Mail, then you're really going to like smart playlists in iTunes.

Smart playlists are very similar to other 'smart' objects – instead of creating a static list of songs, you can create criteria that iTunes will use to create a playlist. For example, you might want to build a playlist from a certain year, or that features a certain artist or has a certain rating or play count. When you build a smart playlist, iTunes adds songs to it automatically and keeps the playlist updated as you grow your music collection.

To create a smart playlist:

1 Choose File > New Smart Playlist from the menu.

2 Choose an item from the first dropdown, such as Artist or Genre.

3 Make appropriate selections from the second and third fields. For example, if you chose Genre, you might choose 'is' from the second dropdown and enter World in the third field.

4 If you have additional criteria, click the + button and add them.

5 Click OK when you've finished.

6 Your new playlist appears in the sidebar. Click the playlist and give it a more appropriate name.

To see the list of songs in a smart playlist, just click on the playlist in the sidebar.

? DID YOU KNOW?
iTunes will create various smart playlists for you. For example, one smart playlist is called Purchased and it contains every song you've purchased from the iTunes Store.

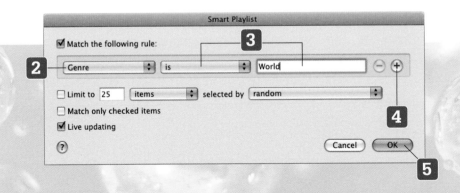

Tip 8: Set up smart folders in Finder

What's a smart folder? It's a folder that you create with certain search criteria. Maybe you want to see all the files you worked on last week. Or maybe you want to see all files labelled with a certain colour that are of a certain type (like photos or music files). Once you build a smart folder, wherever those files are, they'll be found and displayed in the smart folder. If you add more files next week that meet the criteria, you'll get an updated view.

To create a smart folder:

1 Choose File > New Smart Folder in the Finder menu.

2 Click the + button on the far right to add criteria for your new smart folder.

3 For example, select Last opened date and make the criteria yesterday.

4 Save your smart folder with an appropriate name (like Opened Yesterday).

Your new smart folder will show up under Search For on the sidebar.

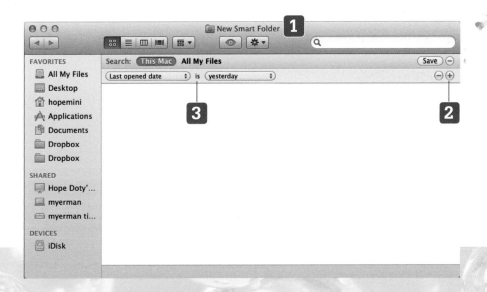

Tip 9: Add folders to the Dock

The Dock is where you keep all your most heavily used applications – each is accessible with a simple click. However, you're not just limited to placing applications in the Dock – you can also add folders to the right side of the Dock.

Why would you want to do this? Well, imagine you've got a set of documents you're constantly working on. Instead of opening a Finder window, you'd be able to just click the folder's icon right on the Dock.

To add a folder to the Dock:

1 Open the Finder.

2 Click the icon for Macintosh HD.

3 Drag the Applications folder to the right side of the Dock. There! Now you have access to every single Mac application right at your fingertips.

4 Control-click the Application folder icon and set it up as a List, which will make it easier to use.

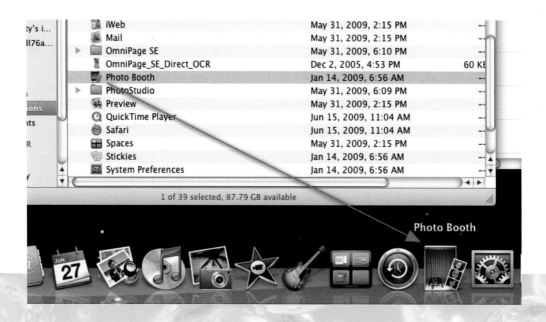

Tip 10: Using Facetime

Mac OS X Lion comes with Facetime installed. What is Facetime? It's a video calling service similar to Skype and other video chat services. Using Facetime, you can video chat with another Facetime user, whether they're sitting in front of a Mac or using an iPhone 4 or iPad 2.

To use Facetime:

1 Click the Facetime icon on your dock.

2 The first time you use Facetime, you will need to register with your Apple ID.

3 To talk with someone, you must know their email address.

4 To call someone, double click their email address or name.

1 Getting started with your new Mac

Introduction

Welcome to the world of Mac! You're in for a delightful computing experience. Macs are known across the world as being supremely easy to use, extremely secure and very resilient. You'll love yours because it's fast, reliable, free from most viruses and can easily be configured to work exactly the way you do.

With Mac OS X, the Mac's powerful operating system, comes a variety of built-in applications that make your Mac immediately useful right out of the box. For example, without having to buy any other software, you can send and receive emails, keep track of all your contacts and addresses, set up a calendar, browse the Web, manage your photographs, listen to music, chat on the Internet, edit your digital movies, build websites and much, much more.

If you're brand new to the world of Macs, this first chapter will get you oriented. You'll learn about the Apple menu, the Desktop, the Dock, the Finder, the Trash and many other useful elements.

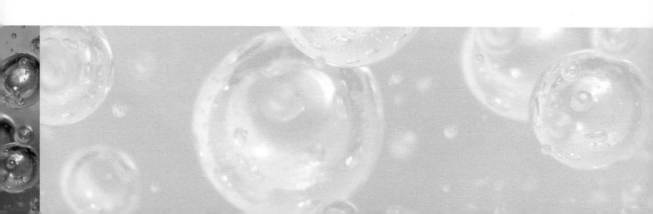

Start your Mac

The brains of your Mac is Mac OS X. It's unlike all the other software on your Mac because it is the operating system – in other words, it's everything the Mac needs to operate systems, everything from files and folders to graphics and sounds and web connectivity. Without its operating system, your Mac would be as useless as a doorstop.

Before you can even use your Mac, you have to start it.

1 If you're working with a MacBook, MacBook Pro or MacBook Air, open the lid.

2 If your Mac was sleeping, you don't have to do anything else. If it was turned off completely, hold down the power button for a second or two.

3 You will see the Apple logo flash on the screen, then the Desktop will appear.

The Desktop

The first thing you'll see when you boot up your Mac is the Desktop. The Desktop is simply a space where you can put files, folders and other applications. Some people prefer to keep their Desktops very clean, others crowd them with files, and still others put only folders and files on them that need immediate attention.

You'll notice a few interesting things about the Desktop. The first is an icon of a hard drive in the upper right-hand side with the label 'Macintosh HD'. This represents your start-up disk – basically, your entire hard drive. In the world of Mac, whenever you attach a thumb drive or download software from the Internet, the underlying operating system will create a new disk to hold it.

Two other items of interest are the Dock, which resides along the bottom of the screen, and the Menu bar, which stretches across the top.

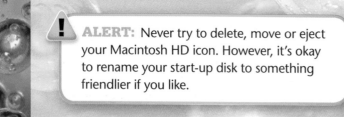

ALERT: Never try to delete, move or eject your Macintosh HD icon. However, it's okay to rename your start-up disk to something friendlier if you like.

Mousing

Most of the time, you'll be using your mouse to get things done. There are a few basic things you need to know about your Apple mouse, primarily that it has one button. Don't despair, though, because it has all the capabilities of other mice and then some.

You have four different ways to interact with your Mac using a mouse:

1 The single-click, in which you click on a file, folder or application.

2 The double-click, in which you click on a file, folder or application in quick succession. This will normally open the item for viewing or editing.

3 The control-click, in which you hold down the ctrl button and the mouse button. This is effectively the same as a right mouse button click and will display a pop-up menu for whatever you're looking at.

4 Click and drag, in which you hold down the mouse button, drag over an area of the screen to highlight various items (such as files or folders) and then release the mouse button.

If you're on a laptop, you have a variety of other functionality available to you via the trackpad. For example, you can drag two fingers at the same time up and down to vertically scroll, and you can set one finger down on the trackpad and then use a second finger to simulate a control-click.

? **DID YOU KNOW?**

If the one-button mouse is too weird for you, simply buy a two-button mouse. Your Mac will use it just fine.

! **ALERT:** In Mac OS X Lion, they've reversed the scrolling on your mouse to be more like swiping on the iPad. If you don't like it, you can always change it by clicking Preferences and going to Mouse, and unchecking 'move content in the direction of finger movement when scrolling or navigating'.

The Menu bar

The Menu bar stretches all the way across the top of your screen and it always contains the menu for the currently available application. If you're ever confused about which application is currently 'active' (or 'on top'), simply take a look at the upper left-hand corner of your Mac's user interface and you'll see the name in bold right next to the little Apple icon.

Menu bar

If you click directly on an open space on the Desktop, you'll see that the display says Finder. You'll learn more about the Finder, but it's basically the way that you browse for files and folders on your Mac. Because the Finder is active, you see the top-level menu items for it in the Menu bar (File, Edit, View, Go, Window and Help).

On the far right side of the Menu bar are several other icons. Depending on what you've got set up, you'll see different icons. For example, on my system I see an icon for Time Machine, Spaces (both of which we'll talk about later), my WiFi signal strength, a volume control, a small US flag to indicate what keyboard I'm using, my remaining battery power, a date and time, and a little magnifying glass that represents Spotlight, the Mac's powerful search facility.

Menu bar icons

The Apple menu

Regardless of which application is active, you'll always be able to see the Apple menu. It lets you have access to various useful tools such as:

- About this Mac (which gives you information about the operating system).
- System Preferences (so you can change different settings).
- Dock Preferences.
- Recent Items.
- Force Quit (in case you need to make a misbehaving application stop working).
- Sleep (to put your Mac to sleep temporarily).
- Restart (to restart your Mac).
- Shut Down (to shut it down for a long period of time).
- Log out (to switch users, if you have more than one user set up on your Mac).

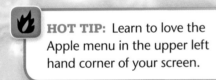

HOT TIP: Learn to love the Apple menu in the upper left hand corner of your screen.

The Dock

The Dock is where you keep your most commonly used applications. Some users pack a lot of applications onto their Docks for convenience sake, others just keep a handful. The important thing to know is that you can add, remove and rearrange applications on the Dock to fit your needs.

Another important thing to know is the divider line on the right side of the Dock. To the left of that line you can place applications. To the right of that line you can put all kinds of interesting things.

For one thing, the Trash lives there, but so can different folders. For example, I've placed a folder that points to the Documents folder that I use. I also have folders that hold a list of all applications on the Mac, as well as a folder that holds recently downloaded documents.

The Dock

? DID YOU KNOW?

You can access additional features by control-clicking an application icon in the Dock. For example, you can control-click the iTunes icon and choose Play from the menu to play a song.

Starting an application

To start an application in the Dock, simply click the appropriate icon. In the example below, I've clicked the Safari icon (the one that looks like a compass) to open up the Safari web browser. Once you open an application, the Dock displays a very small indicator that looks like a light under that icon.

Once an application is open, you will see it open in a window. Along the top of the window is a title pane that shows the name of the document (or, in the case of Safari, the title of the webpage you're looking at) and to the left of that are three little buttons in the upper left corner.

- The red button quits or closes the application.
- The yellow button minimises the application.
- The green button maximises the application.

? DID YOU KNOW?

Whenever the Mac is waiting for you to do something related to an application, that application's icon in the Dock will start bouncing up and down to alert you.

Quitting an application

You can quit an open application in many ways.

- You can click the red icon in the window.
- You can access the main menu for that application. If you've started Safari, you can click the word Safari next to the Apple menu, then click Quit.
- You can type the keyboard shortcut ⌘ Q.
- You can control-click the active application's icon in the Dock and choose Quit from the pop-up menu.

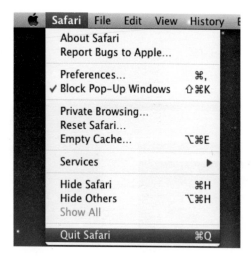

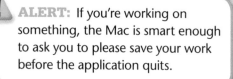

ALERT: If you're working on something, the Mac is smart enough to ask you to please save your work before the application quits.

DID YOU KNOW?
The ⌘ key is next to the space bar and works a lot like the control key in Windows. You'll learn a whole lot of other shortcuts as we go.

Resizing an application

You can resize any application by using your mouse to adjust the lower right-hand corner. This is the only way to resize a window on a Mac, as none of the other corners is draggable.

To resize an application window:

1 Hover your mouse over the lower right-hand corner of the application window.

2 Hold down the mouse button and drag to resize the window.

3 Release the mouse button.

Minimising an application

Sometimes you need to get an application off the screen, but you don't want to stop working with it altogether. Thankfully, your Mac allows you to minimise any application that is running.

To minimise an application, click the yellow icon along the top of the application window.

Notice that the window minimises with a slick animation and then shows up as a tiny icon on the right side of your Dock. Also notice that as you minimise more and more icons, the other icons in the Dock might resize to make room.

To get your minimised application back, all you have to do is click the application's icon on the Dock and it will pop back up in front of you with the same slick animation – but this time in reverse.

Rearranging Dock items

If you're anything like me, you can't stand to leave things as they are. One of the first things you'll want to do is rearrange the application icons on the Dock. For example, you may have some applications that you use more often than others, so you'll move them to the left or right as needed. Or you may want to group icons together.

To rearrange an icon on the Dock:

1 Hover your mouse over the desired icon, then click and hold.

2 Move the icon either left or right, until it's in the position you want it to be.

3 Release your mouse button to place the icon.

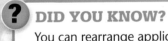

Adding applications to the Dock

Sometimes you want to add or remove applications altogether from the Dock. This is totally OK and actually, it's encouraged. The good folks at Apple know that no two people work exactly the same. In fact, if you got 20 MacBook users together in a room and looked at their Docks, you'd probably see 20 different variations.

To add an application to the Dock:

1 Click the Finder icon on the far left. It looks like a two-tone blue smiley face.

2 On the left sidebar of the Finder, you'll see a list of devices. Click the one that corresponds to your hard drive.

3 Click the Applications folder.

4 If you want to add an application to the Dock, simply drag it from the Applications folder to the Dock.

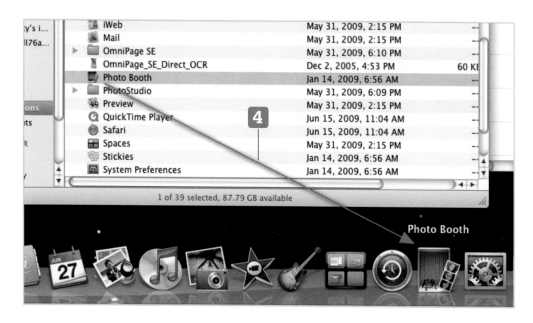

? DID YOU KNOW?

The Dock will actually make space for the new application as its icon gets closer.

! ALERT: If you don't go all the way, you'll end up with the application moved to the Desktop. This isn't necessarily bad, just untidy. Make sure that you're hovering over the Dock before you release the icon.

Removing applications from the Dock

Removing an application from the Dock is very simple.

1 Click and hold down the button on the application icon you want to remove.

2 Drag the icon up and away from the Dock and release the mouse button. You will see a little puff of smoke when this happens and hear a little sound.

? DID YOU KNOW?

Dragging an application icon from the Dock does *not* delete the application from your Mac. It just removes it from the Dock.

The Trash

The Trash is where deleted items go. By default, it lives as an icon on the far right side of your Dock and it cannot be removed from the Dock or moved to another location on the Dock. Apart from that, it is like any other folder on your Mac. It is a simple holding place for any file, folder, application or other item that you have deleted.

By the way, the easiest way to delete an item is to drag it to the Trash. Notice that when you do this for the first time, the Trash icon changes from empty to full.

You can open the Trash by double-clicking the Trash icon. This will open a folder that contains all the deleted items. You can restore items by dragging them from the Trash to the Desktop.

You can empty the Trash (or take it out, whatever you prefer) by control-clicking the Trash icon and choosing Empty Trash from the pop-up menu.

Trash

Empty

Full

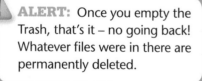

ALERT: Once you empty the Trash, that's it – no going back! Whatever files were in there are permanently deleted.

The Finder

The Finder is a very important application. It might even be the most important application, except it's always there and most people don't stop to think about it being there. Essentially, the Finder is what you use to find files and folders. I'll be devoting an entire chapter to the Finder, but for now let's take a quick tour.

The Finder consists of several panes of information.

- The sidebar contains shortcuts to different disks, devices and folders. You can customise this sidebar to meet your needs.
- The main window shows the content of whatever folder you're looking at.
- To open a folder, document or application, double-click it.
- You can change your view using the buttons along the header bar. You can view files as icons, a list, in column view or in Cover Flow mode (similar to iTunes, more on this later).
- You can run a search by entering a phrase in the search field.

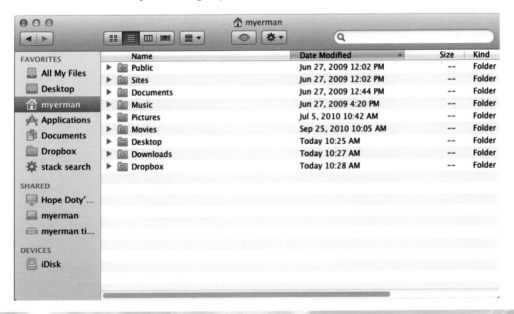

The Home folder

Every Mac is keyed to its user and every user has a Home folder that corresponds to the user name created for it. The Home folder contains some standard folders that you'll be using a lot and you're encouraged to organise your materials here:

- Desktop, which is another view of your Desktop.
- Documents, which holds your spreadsheets, letters and other documents.
- Downloads, which holds any files you download from the Internet.
- Library, which is used by your applications to save settings and other information.
- Movies, which holds your digital movies.
- Music, which holds any iTunes and Garage Band music files.
- Pictures, which holds any photos you have saved.
- Public, which is where you keep any files or folders you're willing to share with others.
- Sites, which contains any websites you create.

Of course, you're free to add other folders, as needed, but the point is: your Home folder is important. Get used to working with it.

? DID YOU KNOW?

Your Mac can support multiple users. Each user can have their own account and their own Home folder.

Basic searches with Spotlight

Sometimes you can't find what you're looking for just with the Finder. For those situations, you need a powerful search utility that will quickly look through every nook and cranny of your system.

No need to look any further, Macs have a powerful search engine called Spotlight built right into them. Spotlight indexes all documents, files, images, music, folders and applications on your Mac. When you do a search for something, it retrieves everything that matches a file name, document name, keywords in metadata and even the file contents themselves.

To start a search, you can do **one** of three things:

1 Click the magnifying glass in the upper right corner of the Menu bar.

2 Enter a phrase directly into the search bar on any Finder window.

3 Press ⌘ and the space bar on the keyboard together.

Doing any of these things will allow you to run a search. In most cases, you'll see the search results return as you type the search phrase. Spotlight will also try to rank the search results, giving you what it thinks is the most probable hit.

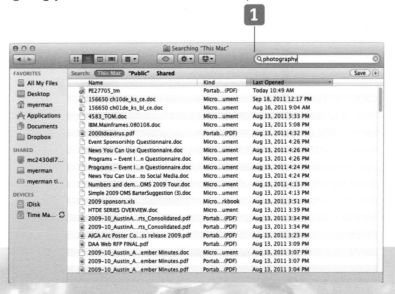

 HOT TIP: You will be using the Spotlight search a lot, mostly because it's much easier and faster than searching for files by hand.

Shutting down or restarting safely

You'll find quickly that your Mac is a very hardy computer. Unlike other computers, it can run for a very long time without needing any kind of shutdown or restart. For example, when I got my first MacBook Pro, I ran it continuously for six months without having to restart it, and I did it only because I felt bad about not restarting it.

However, sometimes you have to perform a manual shutdown or restart. For example, you may need to upgrade some software or the operating system and the last part of the process will require a restart. Or you may need to shut down to protect it from an electrical storm.

To shut down or restart your Mac:

1 Open the Apple menu on the Menu bar by clicking on the Apple icon.

2 To shut down your Mac, choose Shut Down from the menu.

3 To restart your Mac, choose Restart from the menu.

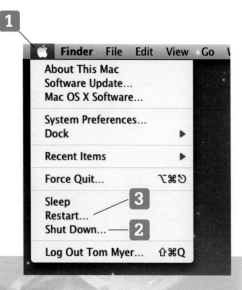

? DID YOU KNOW?

When all else fails, you can shut down your Mac by holding down the power button for a few seconds.

2 Files and folders

Introduction

You'll spend a lot of your time working with files and folders. On the Mac, you work with files and folders through an extremely useful application called the Finder. The Finder is how you browse for files and folders, create and delete files and folders, and how you generally make sense of the file system.

In this chapter, you'll learn not only the basics of the Finder but also all the key functions of working with files and folders. You'll also learn how to label files, compress them, create shortcuts, search for files and save your searches.

Opening the Finder

In Chapter 1 you learned a little bit about the Finder. You learned about the sidebar, the main window, what buttons are available in the headers and how to get good information from the footer.

To open the Finder, you can do **one** of the following:

1 Click the Finder icon in the Dock.

2 Alternatively, click the Desktop and press ⌘ N on the keyboard.

Doing either of these things will open a new Finder window.

Switching to Icon view

Once in the Finder, you have the choice of viewing your files in four different arrangements. The first of these is the Icon view. Viewing your files as a set of thumbnails creates a grid of thumbnails in the main view that gives you a preview of your documents, photos and music files.

Obviously, this kind of view is more useful when dealing with images or other visual materials, but it can also be useful when dealing with a multitude of files.

To switch to Icon view while in the Finder, do **one** of the following:

1 Click the Icon button in the header.

2 Control-click in the main window and choose View > as Icons from the pop-up menu.

3 Choose View > as Icons from the Finder menu.

4 Press ⌘ 1 on the keyboard.

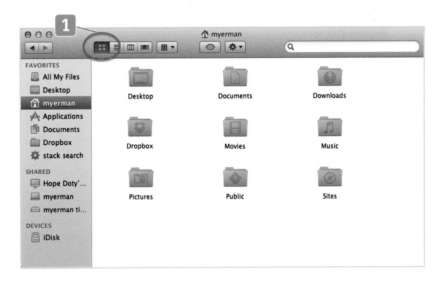

Switching to List view

As useful as the thumbnail view may be, sometimes you need more details about a file than just a preview and a file name. Sometimes you need to know a little more about a file before you can identify it.

The button next to the Icon view button is the List view button. The List view provides you with more information about each file or folder. You get columns for the file/folder name, the date it was last modified, its size in KB or MB, and what type of object it is (folder, image, document and so on).

To switch to List view while in the Finder, do **one** of the following:

1 Click the List button in the header.

2 Control-click in the main window and choose View > as List from the pop-up menu.

3 Choose View > as List from the Finder menu.

4 Press ⌘ 2 on the keyboard.

 HOT TIP: After a while, you'll probably use the numbered keyboard shortcuts: ⌘ 1 for Icon view, ⌘ 2 for List view and so on.

Switching to Column view

So far, so good. If you're coming from the Windows world, thumbnail and list views aren't much different from what you're used to. But now comes something really nice – the Finder's Column view, an incredibly useful way to navigate nested folders.

The Column view presents you with a series of columns that lets you traverse a hierarchy of folders. Make a selection in one column and a new column appears to the right with that selection's content in it.

- If you select a folder, you'll see all the folders and files that live in that folder in the next column.
- If you select a file, you'll see a preview of the selected file and various tidbits of information about that file (like its name, file type, size, creation date, dimensions and so on).

To switch to Column view while in the Finder, do **one** of the following:

1 Click the Column button in the header.

2 Control-click in the main window and choose View > as Columns from the pop-up menu.

3 Choose View > as Columns from the Finder menu.

4 Press ⌘ 3 on the keyboard.

 HOT TIP: Double-clicking a column's drag handle will set its width to match the contents of the column.

 DID YOU KNOW?
Columns can be resized. Just drag the handles at the bottom of each column.

Switching to Cover Flow view

If you're familiar with the iPod or iPhone, you know that the iTunes software on those devices allows you to browse through songs in Cover Flow mode. Essentially, you can see an album cover or other art associated with a song and traverse the list of songs by going forwards or backwards.

Cover Flow in Finder works the same way. You can see a large preview pane at the top and a list of details for each file and folder below. As you traverse the list of objects, the display updates, allowing you to see thumbnail shots of images and documents. It's a fast, intuitive way to find what you're looking for.

To switch to Cover Flow view while in the Finder, do **one** of the following:

1 Click the Cover Flow button in the header.

2 Control-click in the main window and choose View > as Cover Flow from the pop-up menu.

3 Choose View > as Cover Flow from the Finder menu.

4 Press ⌘ 4 on the keyboard.

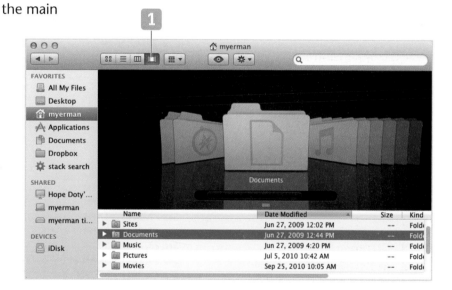

DID YOU KNOW?
You can play movies directly inside Cover Flow.

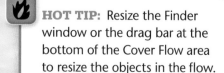
HOT TIP: Resize the Finder window or the drag bar at the bottom of the Cover Flow area to resize the objects in the flow.

Sorting files and folders

Regardless of which view you use (and you'll probably use different views at different times), you will eventually need to sort the display of items in the Finder window.

If you're in Icon view, you'll use the Arrange feature. To arrange icons, you can:

1 Control-click the main Finder window and choose an option under the Keep Arranged By option (for example, by name, date modified, size, kind or label).

If you're in List or Cover Flow view, you can click the header fields at the top of each column. Each header acts as a sort toggle. If the current sort is ascending (A–Z) then clicking it will change the sorting to descending (Z–A) and vice versa.

Getting information on a file or folder

Sometimes you need some detailed information on a file or folder, more than you can get from a listing in the Finder. Luckily for you, the Finder comes with such a feature.

If you need information on any file or folder, simply select that file and take **one** of the following actions:

1 Control-click and choose Get Info from the pop-up menu.

2 Choose File > Get Info from the Finder menu.

3 Press ⌘ I on the keyboard.

The result is an information window that shows you general information about the file, any Spotlight comments you may have entered (like keywords), file size, dimensions (if it's an image), a preview, its sharing and permissions settings and much more.

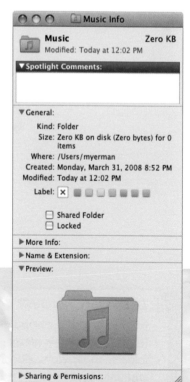

Creating folders

Sometimes you need to create folders to help organise your files, documents, music and photos. After all, your Mac is yours and you need to make it your own.

Creating folders on your desktop or on the Finder is very easy to do. Taking **any** of the following actions will create a folder:

1 Control-click on any blank space in the Finder (or on the Desktop) and select New Folder from the pop-up menu.

2 Select File > New Folder from the Finder menu.

3 Press Shift ⌘ N on the keyboard.

4 Click the Action button (to the right of the Cover Flow button) and choose New Folder.

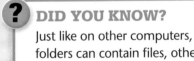

DID YOU KNOW?

Just like on other computers, folders can contain files, other folders, applications, documents and data of all kinds.

Renaming files or folders

Renaming a file or folder is also pretty intuitive on a Mac. All you have to do is:

1 Click a file or folder, then wait for the name to change background colour.

2 Enter a new name or edit the one that is already there.

3 Click outside the name.

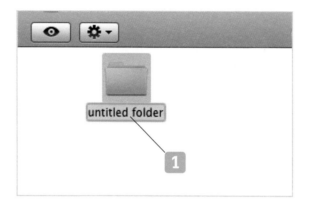

? **DID YOU KNOW?**

Your Mac supports file names up to 255 characters long, including spaces. The only character you can't use in a filename is the colon (:) character. You also can't normally start a filename with a full stop (.) – you have to be an administrator to create a so-called dot-file.

Moving files and folders

Sometimes files get put in the wrong places. Or sometimes you're happy to work with files in a temporary location (such as the Desktop) but then need to move them to a more permanent location.

To move files or folders:

1 Select one or more files or folders.

2 Once selected, drag them to the new destination.

You may need to open a new Finder window if you're moving items to a completely different part of the file system.

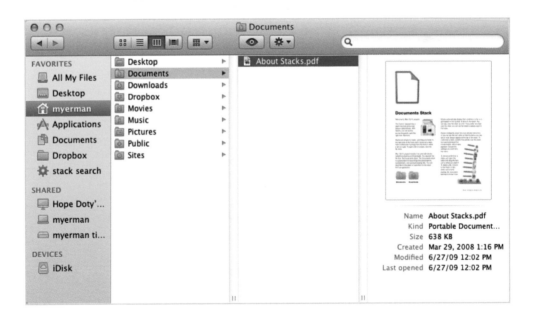

Duplicating files and folders

You'll find you need to make copies of files and folders. Sometimes you may want to have a backup of some files in case you make a mistake. For example, if you're working with digital photographs, you'll want to make a backup copy in case you crop a photo wrongly or make some other mistake.

To duplicate files and folders, select one or more files or folders and do **either** of the following:

1 Press ⌘ C to copy them, then open a new Finder window, navigate to your destination and press ⌘ V to paste them.

2 You can also control-click and select Duplicate from the pop-up menu. This will create duplicate files in the same folder that you can then manipulate. They'll have slightly different names.

? DID YOU KNOW?

If you're copying to an external thumb drive or a backup drive, all you have to do is drag the files and folders as though you're moving them. Your Mac is smart enough to know that you're making a copy.

Deleting files and folders

During the course of your work and play, you may end up with files and folders you no longer want or need. As with other computers, your Mac gives you various options for dealing with unwanted and unneeded items.

To delete a file or folder, you can do **any** of the following:

1 Drag a file or folder to the Trash.

2 Select a file or folder and select File > Move to Trash from the Finder menu.

3 Control-click a file or folder and select Move to Trash from the pop-up menu.

4 Select a file or folder, then press the ⌘ button and Delete button at the same time.

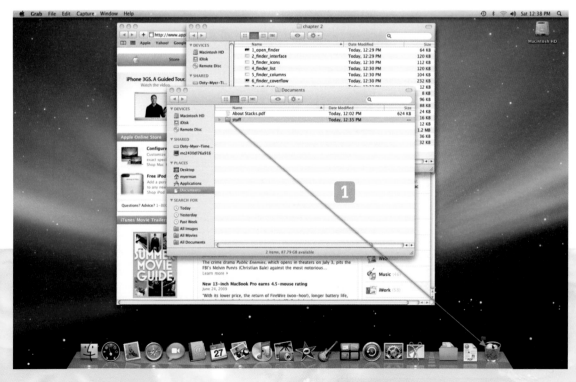

Taking a Quick Look

Sometimes you'll find yourself in a strange situation. You have a whole pile of files to sort through, but they've got weird naming conventions, or you're otherwise not sure what's in the files. The standard way of doing things is to open each file one at a time until you've found what you're looking for. Of course, you may not have the time or patience for that approach, but you still don't really have a clue which file contains what.

Luckily for you, your Mac offers a Quick Look feature. Think of it as a smart preview function.

In order to preview a file with Quick Look, do **one** of the following:

1 Select a file or folder and select File > Quick Look from the Finder menu.

2 Alternatively, press ⌘ Y on the keyboard.

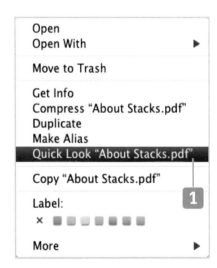

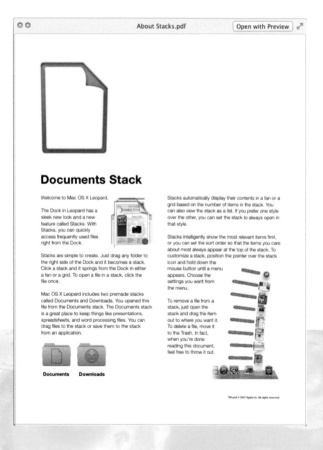

? DID YOU KNOW?

The Quick Look feature is also available to you in Mail, where you can use it to get a sneak peek at attachments.

Labelling files

The Finder lets you organise your files in different ways. Sometimes the best way to organise your files is to stick them in different folders. If you're coming from the Windows world, this is a natural way to work that you're probably used to.

However, the Finder also lets you label your files. You can choose up to seven different coloured labels that you can apply to a file or folder. What's the point? Well, let's say that you have a bunch of files that you need to review. Some of them are photos, others are letters and some others are spreadsheets. Why not give them a red label, as long as you know that 'red' means 'must review'? Or you could use a blue label to indicate that a file or folder is ready to be sent to your boss or friend. The possibilities are endless, and it's really up to you how you use labels.

You can label a file in two different ways. Once you select a file or folder you can do **one** of the following:

1 Control-click your selected file(s) or folder(s) and choose a label colour from the pop-up menu.

2 Alternatively, choose a label colour from the File menu of the Finder menu.

Compressing files and folders

You may want to email a set of files or folders to someone else, or put them on a thumb drive. However, if your files are too big, they probably won't make for very friendly (or portable) attachments.

You can solve this problem by using the built-in compression tools on your Mac. You can simply select a group of files or folders, compress them and your Mac will create a compressed ZIP archive for you.

To compress a group of selected files or folders:

1 Control-click your selection and choose Compress from the pop-up menu.

2 Alternatively, choose File > Compress from the Finder menu.

? DID YOU KNOW?

If you select one file, Finder will create a ZIP using the file's original name but with .zip added to the end of the filename. If more than one file is selected, the resulting archive will be called Archive.zip, unless there's already an Archive.zip in the directory. If that's the case the Finder will create an Archive2.zip, Archive3.zip and so on.

Creating an alias

If you're used to working in Windows, then you're probably familiar with the concept of a shortcut. You might have a document in one area, but you want a shortcut of that file on your Desktop. The shortcut on the Desktop isn't the file itself, just another way to get to the file.

Well, your Mac calls these shortcuts an alias, mostly because that's what they're called in the UNIX world, and at its very heart your Mac is a UNIX machine. An alias can be a very handy thing indeed because it allows you to keep one copy of a file but there are many different ways to get to that file from different locations.

To create an alias:

1 Select a file or folder you want to work with.

2 Control-click your selection and choose Make Alias from the pop-up menu. The result is a new file with the same name as your original file or folder but with the word alias at the end of the filename.

3 Drag that alias where you need it (such as the Desktop).

4 To access the file the alias points to, simply double-click the alias.

About Stacks.pdf alias ———— 4

Searching in Finder

If you're working with a large number of files, sometimes it's good to have powerful search capabilities at your fingertips. Manually checking through a bunch of folders isn't a lot of fun, especially if you're up against a deadline or in a hurry.

Fortunately, each Finder window comes with its own search bar. To run a search:

1 Click inside the search bar.

2 Type your search phrase.

3 The Finder window updates with files and folders that match your search phrase.

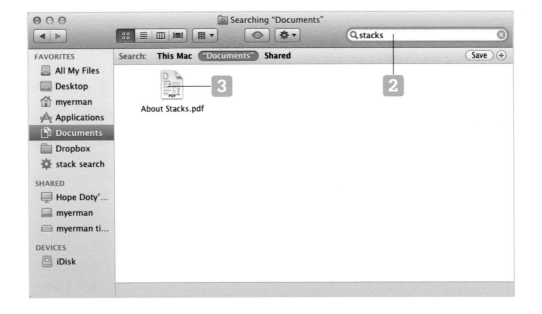

? DID YOU KNOW?

You can change the scope of the search by limiting the search to either contents or filenames, or to the entire Mac or just the folder you're in.

Saving searches in the sidebar

Running a search once is pretty good, but what if you're constantly running the same search over and over again? What if you find yourself dealing with the same set of images, music files, documents or spreadsheets all day long?

Well, did you notice when you ran a search that you had a save button on the far right, next to a little plus sign? You can use the save button to save your search and you can use the plus sign to make modifications to your search to make it more useful.

To modify and save your search:

1 Click the + sign to reveal more options.

2 You can add criteria to limit the types of files you work with, their modification dates, their labels and much more.

3 When you're happy with your search results, press the save button.

4 Give your new search an appropriate name and save it in the Saved Searches folder of your library.

5 Your new search will appear in the Finder sidebar under Search For, ready for you to use again.

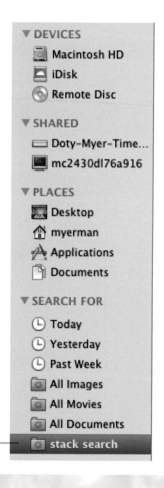

Creating smart folders

You already know all about folders. You create them where you need them, you put files and other items in them, and you keep your life and work organised.

However, sometimes you can't anticipate certain things. For example, you might have files scattered all over your Mac that pertain to a certain topic, but they really do belong in all those other folders because each folder is designated to a certain project.

If you wanted to see all these files and folders in one place, you could build an alias for each and every one of them, but that doesn't seem like a good use of your time. A better idea is to use a smart folder.

To create a smart folder:

1 Choose File > New Smart Folder in the Finder menu.

2 Click the + button on the far right to add criteria for your new smart folder.

3 For example, select Last Opened Date and make the criterion Yesterday.

4 Save your smart folder with an appropriate name (like 'Opened Yesterday').

Your new smart folder will show up under Search For on the sidebar.

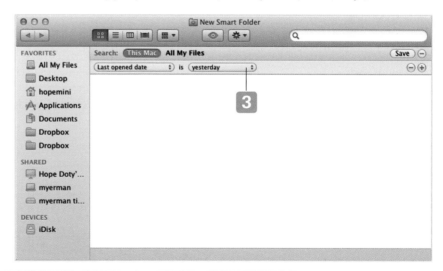

Customising the Finder toolbar

As you get to know your Mac, you'll find yourself going to the same files, folders and applications over and over again. You'll find yourself wanting shortcuts to get to those destinations. Luckily for you, the Finder lets you drag items to the sidebar and the top toolbar. You can also add other features to your toolbar as needed.

Once dragged to the sidebar or toolbar, a file, folder or application becomes a shortcut icon to that destination.

To add a file or folder to the sidebar or the toolbar:

1 Select a file or folder.

2 Drag it to the sidebar/ toolbar under Places.

You now have access to that file or folder.

To change anything about your toolbar:

3 Control-click anywhere on the toolbar and choose Customize Toolbar from the pop-up menu.

4 You can add various components to the toolbar (such as Quick Look or Delete), designate what gets shown as toolbar buttons (icons only, icons and labels, labels only) or drag a default set of buttons and tools.

5 Click Done when you've finished.

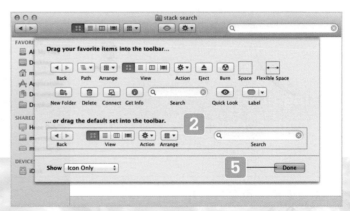

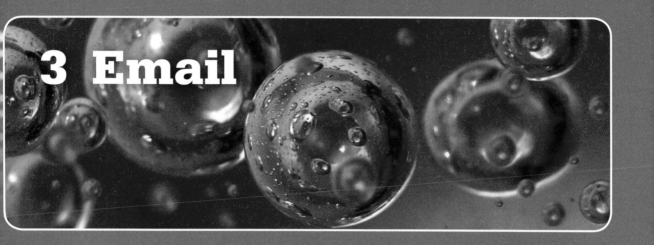

3 Email

Introduction

One of the first things you'll probably want to do once you get your new Mac is to send an email to all your friends and family telling them about your shiny new computer. It's a good thing that each Mac comes with a free email application called Mail.

Mail is a versatile, easy-to-use and fast email application that allows you to send and receive emails, work with attachments, organise your emails, search emails with lightning speed, take notes, create to-do lists and much more.

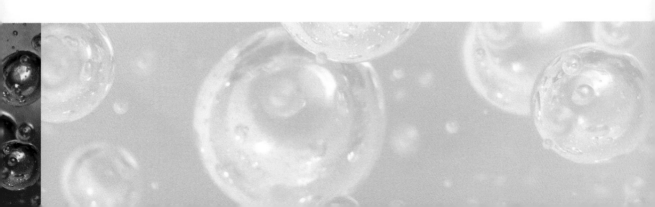

Starting Mail

Before you can send or receive emails, you need to start Mail.

- The easiest way to start Mail is to click the Mail icon in the Dock.
- You can also open a Finder window, navigate to the Applications folder and double-click the Mail icon.

When you open Mail, you'll see the following:

- A toolbar along the top with a variety of buttons that lets you get mail, compose a new message, delete mail, reply to mail and search.
- A sidebar that lists your mailboxes, reminders and folders.
- A preview pane that lists any and all message headers.

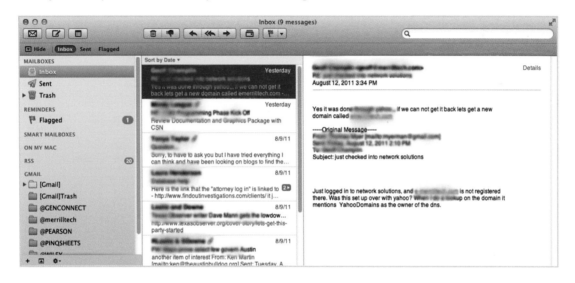

? DID YOU KNOW?

You can easily tell how many unread emails are in your inbox by looking at the Mail icon in the Dock. The little number on the icon indicates how many new emails you have.

Setting up an account

The first thing you'll need to do is configure your settings. After all, there's no sense in having an email application if you can't actually send or receive email.

The first step in setting up your email is to connect to a mail server. You do that by opening the Preferences menu on Mail. To open the Preferences menu, do one of the following:

- Press the ⌘ and comma (,) buttons on the keyboard together.
- Choose Preferences from the Mail menu.

Once you're in the Preferences menu:

1 Click the Accounts tab.

2 Click the + button to add a new account.

3 Give your new account a name, like 'Gmail' or 'Suzie's Mail'.

4 Enter your email address and name.

5 Enter the address of the incoming mail server, your account user name and password.

6 Enter the information for the outgoing mail server by clicking the dropdown next to Outgoing Mail Server (SMTP) and adding your information.

7 When you've finished, just close the Preferences window. Your work is automatically saved for you.

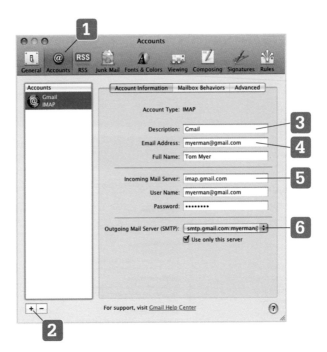

HOT TIP: You can get all of this information from your ISP. Please contact them if you have any questions.

? DID YOU KNOW?

You can use either POP or IMAP to get your email. POP is retrieved from the server and put on your Mac, while IMAP stays on the server, allowing you to access your mailbox from many different devices.

Setting up a signature

If you're like most people who use email, you'll probably want to add a signature file to the end of your emails. A signature file can contain any information at all really, but typically it contains your contact information: your name, email address, mobile phone number and other important information (and sometimes a silly quotation or other personal note).

To set up a signature file:

1 Press the ⌘ and comma (,) buttons on the keyboard together or choose Preferences from the Mail menu.

2 Click the Signatures tab.

3 Click the + button to add a new signature.

4 Create your signature by typing in the edit window.

5 You can choose to match the font in the message by ticking the box under the edit window.

Your new signature appears in the list of signatures to the left. Your first signature is always named Signature #1, but you can rename it by clicking on it and then entering a new name.

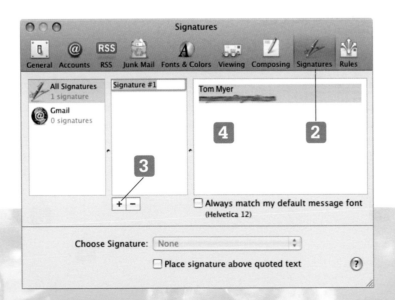

Composing an email

The first thing you'll want to do after setting up an account and a signature is to send your first email. Sending emails with Mail is a fairly easy thing to do, as you would expect with this kind of tool.

To send an email, you can do one of the following:

- Click the New Message button on the Mail toolbar.
- Choose File > New Message from the menu.
- Press ⌘ N on the keyboard.

The result is always the same: a new email window opens up. Once open, you can:

1 Add recipients on the To: line.

2 Add a subject.

3 Compose a message body.

4 Add one or more attachments by clicking the Attachments button.

5 Assign an importance to a message by selecting one from the dropdown.

6 Assign a signature to your note by choosing one from the dropdown.

7 Click the Send button.

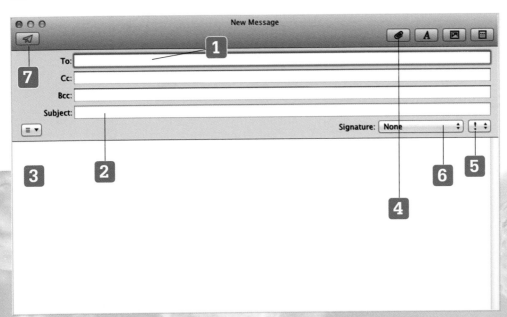

Using Cc and Bcc correctly

Like most other email applications, Mail allows you to copy (Cc) and blind-copy (Bcc) recipients. If you're not familiar with these terms, here's a quick rundown:

- When you Cc a group of people, everyone can see who has been copied on the original message. For example, if you send an email to Tom and copy Joe and Bill, all three of them can see everyone who's been copied on the message.
- When you Bcc an individual or group, nobody can see who is on the Bcc list. If you send a message to Tom and Cc Joe and Bill, then Bcc Susan, nobody on the list will know that Susan has been copied. Of course, Susan will be able to see that Tom, Joe and Bill all got a copy of the email.

To Cc someone on an email, all you have to do is add their email address to the Cc field. You can separate a list of recipients with commas: joe@example.com, bill@example.com, and so on.

To Bcc someone on an email, you need to take the following steps:

1 The Bcc field won't be visible until you click the configuration dropdown below the Subject line and tick Bcc Address Field.

2 Once the Bcc field is in place, add recipient email addresses there as needed, separating each address with a comma.

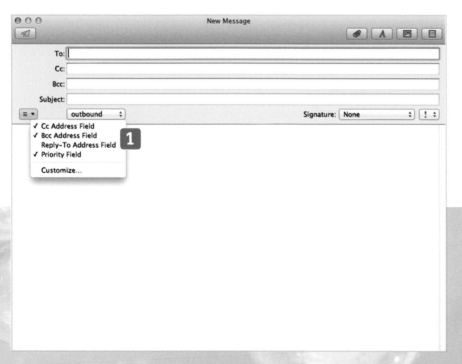

Adding an attachment

Most of the time, writing a quick note to a friend, colleague or family member will do just fine. Other times, you'll want to send along some kind of document – whether a Word document, image, archive or some other file.

Mail, like most other email applications, supports the use of attachments. To add an attachment to an email message, you can do **one** of the following:

- Drag a file into the message window.
- Click the Attachment button and then browse to select the file you want to attach.

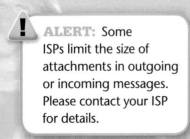

ALERT: Some ISPs limit the size of attachments in outgoing or incoming messages. Please contact your ISP for details.

Viewing an attachment

In Chapter 2 you learned about the Quick Look feature of Finder. You learned that you could use it to get a quick preview of lots of different files – not just images, but word-processing files, spreadsheets, PDFs and many others.

You'll be happy to know that you have the same functionality available to you in Mail. If you receive an email with an attachment, there's no need to open the attachment when you can use Quick Look.

To use Quick Look:

1 Open an email that contains an attachment.

2 Click the Quick Look button next to the Save button.

The Quick Look application will give you a preview of each of your attachments in order. It's a quick and easy way to determine what content is in the attachments without having to open them first.

? DID YOU KNOW?

Sometimes sending attachments from a Mac to a Windows user can cause problems. To solve this problem, choose Edit > Attachments > Always Send Windows-Friendly Attachments from the menu.

Saving attachments

Of course, if someone sends you an email with an attachment, you probably want to save some of those files to your Mac. That way, if someone sends you a document, image, music file or archive, you can put them on your Desktop or your folder for future processing or work.

To save an attachment, first open an email message that contains one or more attachments, then do **one** of the following:

1 Click the Save button in the header of the email. This will save all attachments to the Downloads folder in your Home folder.

2 Click the arrow button next to Attachments to reveal a list of attachments. Simply drag each file one at a time to the Desktop or a Finder window.

3 Choose File > Save Attachments from the menu. This will save all attachments to the Downloads folder in your Home folder.

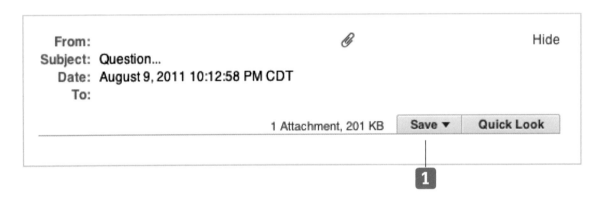

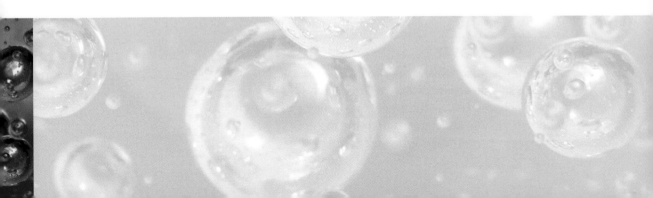

Getting new email

Once you've sent a few emails, chances are you'll start receiving them too – either because people are responding to your messages or just writing their own missives to you.

By default, Mail knows to retrieve mail every once in a while – usually every minute or so. You can also manually retrieve email by doing **one** of the following:

1 Click the Get Mail button on the toolbar.

2 Alternatively, choose Mail > Get New Mail from the menu.

If there's new mail for you on the server, it will show up in your inbox and you'll see a small counter next to the Inbox label in the sidebar to indicate how many unread messages you have.

DID YOU KNOW?

You can change how often Mail retrieves email messages. You'll learn how to do that on the next page.

Changing how often mail is retrieved

By default, Mail will automatically check email every minute. For some, this won't be a problem at all; for others, this many interruptions in a day (that's almost 500 in an eight-hour workday) can lead to insanity. If you're working on a project that requires a lot of concentration, the last thing you need is constant reminders that people want to bug you.

Never fear, though, because you can easily change how often mail is retrieved (even setting it to manual only):

1 Press the ⌘ and comma (,) buttons on the keyboard together or choose Preferences from the Mail menu.

2 Click the General tab.

3 On the Check for new mail dropdown, choose the right frequency for you. You can set the frequency to every minute, every 5 minutes, every 15 minutes, every 30 minutes and every hour, as well as setting it at manual only.

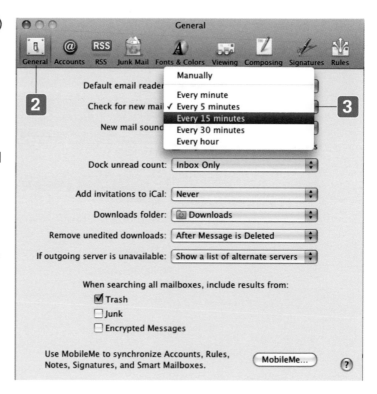

? DID YOU KNOW?

You can set which sounds you hear when you get new email by choosing a sound from the New mail sound dropdown. You can also set it to None, which is my favourite setting!

Creating mailboxes (folders) in Mail

If you're like most users, your email inbox soon gets pretty full and you need to do something with it all.

Like most email applications, Mail lets you create nested folders to help you keep your emails organised. You can create folders with just about any naming convention, using spaces, numbers or special symbols in those names. You can also nest your folders as deep as you need to in order to stay organised.

Here's the catch though: in Mail, folders are called mailboxes. But don't let that throw you off!

To create a new folder, you can do **either** of the following:

1 Click the + button on the bottom of the sidebar and select New Mailbox.

2 Alternatively, choose File > New Mailbox from the menu.

Once created, your new mailbox/folder appears in the sidebar. Just click it to access the emails in that folder.

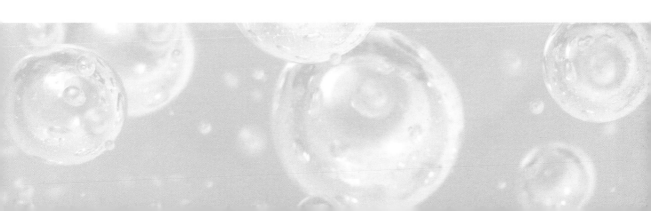

Creating smart mailboxes

In Chapter 2 you learned about smart folders in the Finder. A smart folder, if you'll recall, is a folder that contains a set of criteria for finding files that go in it. If you want to track all files created on a certain date, with a certain label or with a certain filename or extension, then you could build a smart folder for it.

A smart mailbox is the same idea, but applied to your email. How can this be useful? Imagine being able to quickly find:

- all emails with a certain subject line;
- all emails from a certain group of people;
- all emails you received last week that were marked important;
- all emails you received last week with attachments;
- all emails you sent to a certain person.

A smart mailbox will find emails that match its search criteria no matter where they actually live in Mail. This makes it an ideal solution for those who like to tuck their emails into nested folders but still need ready access to them.

To create a smart mailbox, either:

1 Click the + button at the bottom of the sidebar and choose New Smart Mailbox from the menu.

2 Alternatively, choose Mailbox > New Smart Mailbox from the menu.

Once you do either of these, give your new smart mailbox an appropriate name and then use the + button to add criteria to your smart mailbox. For example, to always see email you've received in the past three days but haven't replied to:

1 Name the smart mailbox 'Last 3 Days Unreplied Mail'.

2 Choose Date Received from the first dropdown.

3 Choose 'is in the last' from the second dropdown.

4 Enter a 3 in the text field.

5 Click the + button.

6 Choose Message was not Replied to in the dropdown.

7 Click OK.

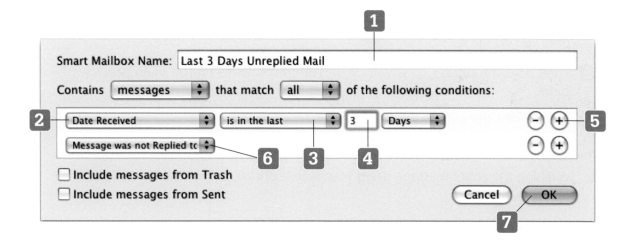

? DID YOU KNOW?

To include sent messages or messages you've deleted, simply tick the boxes next to these options.

Searching for email

In Chapters 1 and 2, you learned about Spotlight and how it is available by pressing ⌘ space and also as a search bar in the Finder. Guess what? Other applications also have their own search bars and Mail is no exception.

If you're used to working with other email applications, you know how tedious it can be to find certain emails. You might remember that it was from a particular person, or that it had a certain subject line, or that it had an attachment or arrived on a certain day. However, without a good search function, you might find yourself digging in your email for hours without finding what you need.

You don't have to worry about any of that when you use Mail. Its search functionality is as powerful as anything available with Spotlight because, well, it is Spotlight.

To run a search of your email:

1 Click in the search bar. If you can't see the search bar, make the Mail window wider until you do see it.

2 Enter a search phrase. This will cause search results to fill the main preview pane.

You can change the scope of the search by:

- Searching in all mailboxes (or just the mailbox you were originally in, like the inbox).
- Searching the entire message using your search phrase, or just the From, To or Subject lines.

? DID YOU KNOW?

You can save your searches as smart mailboxes by clicking the Save button. That way your most common searches are available for reuse later!

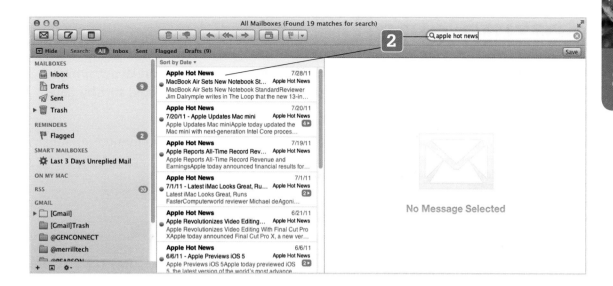

HOT TIP: Click the little x icon in the search bar to remove your search phrase and the search results.

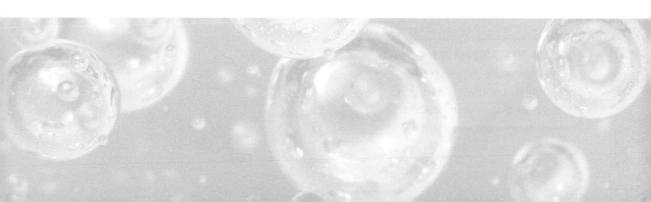

Sorting email

Previous to Mac OS X Lion, Mail used to display messages in a column layout similar to the Finder. To sort mail, you could simply click a column and it would sort by date, subject, or sender.

● In the new Mail, you sort mail by choosing View > Sort By from the menu.

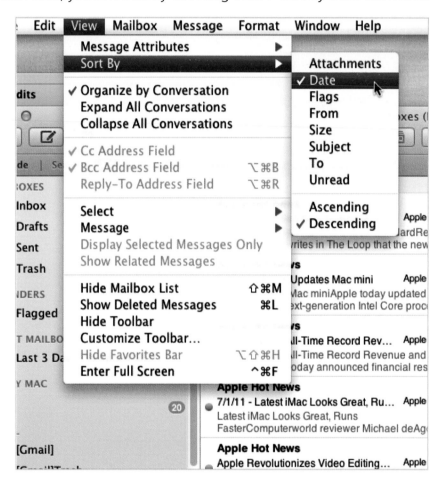

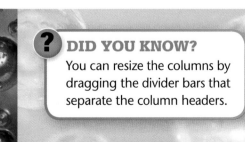

DID YOU KNOW?

You can resize the columns by dragging the divider bars that separate the column headers.

Changing columns in an email listing

Sometimes the standard email columns aren't enough to let you get your work done. For example, you might need to see if a file has an attachment, or you may want to reorder the columns in the view.

To add or remove columns:

1 Choose View > Message Attributes from the menu.

2 To add columns to the display, tick the ones you want to see.

3 To remove columns from the display, untick the ones you no longer want to see.

To change the order of the columns:

1 Click and drag a column header to the left or right.

2 When the column header is in the place you want it, release the mouse button.

Customising the toolbar

Mail's toolbar contains a variety of useful buttons and tools (like the search bar) to keep you working efficiently. However, you may want to add a few things (and take away a few other things!) to make it work the way you want it to.

Thankfully, Mail allows you to customise the toolbar. To configure the toolbar:

1 Control-click somewhere on the toolbar and choose Customize Toolbar. Your best bet is to control-click on a bit of open space between buttons.

2 A window opens that displays a series of buttons and tools. You can drag a default set onto the toolbar or drag individual elements, such as:

- a print button;
- an Address Book button;
- separators;
- a Chat button.

3 Click Done when you've finished.

What you add to your toolbar is up to you, of course, and how you use Mail.

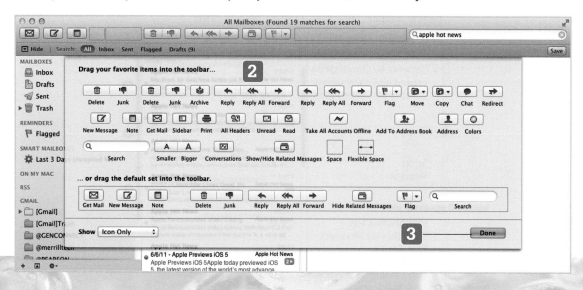

Creating notes in Mail

Mail isn't just about email. Mail also lets you create other types of information, such as notes and to-do lists.

A note is just what you think it is: a document that you use to jot down your thoughts, some meeting minutes or any other notes about a project, event or activity. Notes are saved in your inbox and can be forwarded or sent like any other email, making them pretty useful.

To create a note, you can do **one** of the following:

1 Choose File > New Note from the menu.

2 Alternatively, click the Note button on the toolbar (if you've added it).

When you take either of these actions, you'll see a new note appear – it will look like a yellow legal note pad. You can type your words directly in your note, add attachments and then send it to someone.

Once saved, notes are available under the Notes section of the sidebar. Each note can be accessed by clicking directly on it, as you would with any email.

? DID YOU KNOW?

You can change the fonts and colours of any text in a note.

Flagging mail

During the course of your emailing, you are bound to get some email that you'll consider extremely important. The email may contain special attachments, remind you about a TV show that you must watch or contain some useful bit of information for an upcoming project.

Mail has an easy way for you to designate those emails as important: it's called flagging. When you flag an email, Mail not only attaches a little flag icon to the message, it also makes it easy for you to create smart mailboxes that let you track flagged messages.

To flag a message, you can do **one** of the following:

1 Select one or more mail messages and click the Flag button on the toolbar (if you've added it).

2 Select one or more mail messages and choose Message > Mark > As Flagged from the menu.

3 Select one or more mail messages and press the Shift ⌘ L keys on the keyboard.

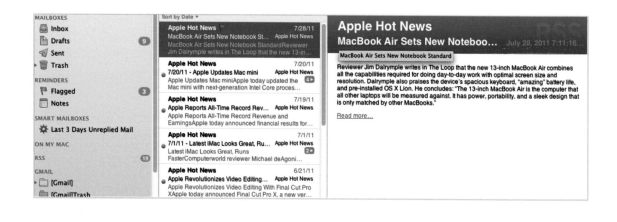

 HOT TIP: You can unflag a flagged piece of mail by selecting it and clicking the Unflag button on the toolbar.

Printing mail

Sometimes you need to keep a paper trail. Maybe someone has sent you an important note, a poem, a grocery list or some other bit of information important enough to print out.

You can print any email in any mailbox (smart or otherwise) by following these steps:

1 Select the email you want to print.

2 Choose Print from the File menu or press the ⌘ P keys on the keyboard.

3 Make your final selections on the print dialogue.

4 Click Print when you've finished.

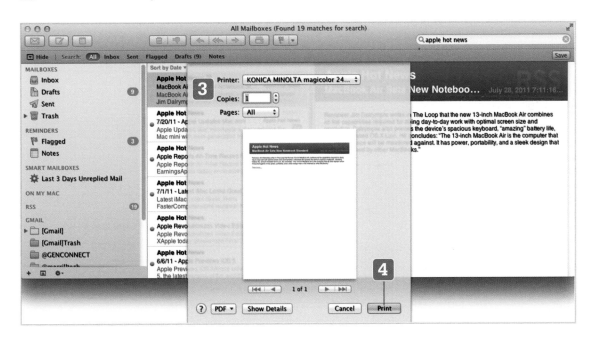

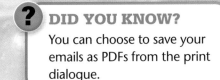

DID YOU KNOW?

You can choose to save your emails as PDFs from the print dialogue.

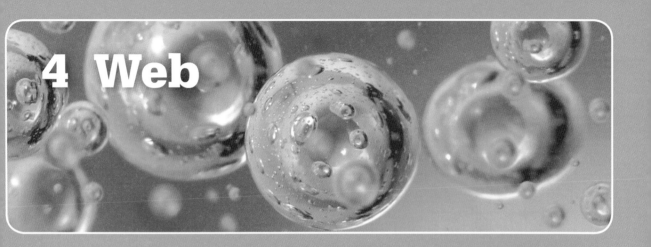

4 Web

Introduction

If you're like a lot of users, you'll spend a great deal of your time surfing the Web, downloading files, reading blogs, writing comments on others' blogs, and other fun activities.

Your Mac comes with a free Web browser called Safari. If you've ever used Firefox, then you'll find Safari to be pretty similar. It's fast, secure and comes with an impressive array of features that allows you to view multiple websites at once (using tabs), subscribe to RSS feeds, save and organise bookmarks, block Web ads and a lot more.

Starting Safari

Before you can do anything on the Web, you need to start Safari.

The easiest way is to click the Safari icon on the Dock. It looks like a blue compass.

Once you've got Safari open, take a moment to orient yourself.

1 Along the top is a toolbar with various buttons that help you navigate the Web, including a URL field and a search bar.

2 Unlike other Mac applications, the search bar doesn't search your Mac, it uses Google to search the Web.

3 Below the toolbar is the Bookmarks bar. You can place your most common bookmarks here for easy access.

4 Below that is the browser pane, which is where requested webpages get rendered.

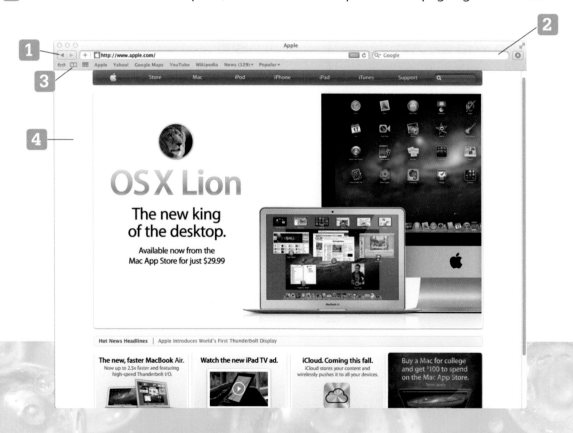

Opening a Web destination

The first thing you'll want to do is go to a webpage. When you first open Safari, you'll probably end up on www.apple.com/startpage. However, you're free to navigate to any page that you might know the address to.

To go directly to a webpage:

1 Click in the URL field in the toolbar.

2 Type the URL for your destination.

3 Press return on the keyboard.

2

+ 🌐 www.google.com ↻

? DID YOU KNOW?
Web addresses are known as URLs – uniform resource locators. Each one is a unique destination or page on the Internet.

🔥 HOT TIP: You can normally leave off the http:// part of the address, as Safari will do its best to figure that part out.

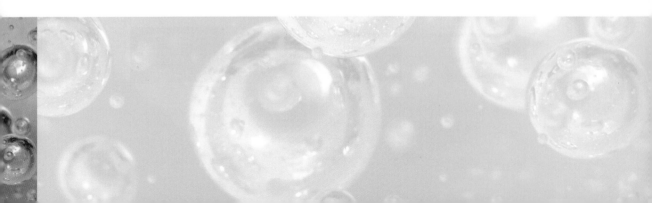

Searching the Web with Safari

Knowing about a particular website address is nice, but when you're first starting out, or if you're trying to find some information, you don't have anything to go with. What you need is access to a fast, reliable search engine.

Luckily for you, Safari has Google searches built right into the browser. Yes, you could go to google.com to run your searches, but as a Safari user, you don't have to.

To run a search in Safari:

1 Click the search bar in the upper right corner of the browser.

2 Type in your search phrase.

3 Press return on the keyboard.

As soon as you press return, your search phrase is sent to Google and then Safari displays a set of search results that match your search phrase. Just click any of the links to open those webpages.

 **DID YOU KNOW?**

You're free to visit any of the other search engines out there, like Yahoo for example. However, only the Google search engine is integrated with Safari.

Creating bookmarks

Often you'll find yourself visiting a particular website or even an interesting page on that website and will want to return to that site over and over. You might have a really great memory and try to keep a list of favourite websites in your head, but for most of us this won't be possible.

Fortunately, you don't have to. Like most other major browsers, Safari lets you bookmark websites. A bookmark is just a simple reminder, a link if you will, to a website. It consists of a name for the site you're interested in and its unique Web address.

To create a bookmark, you can do **one** of the following:

1 Click the + button on the toolbar.

2 Press ⌘ D on the keyboard.

3 Choose Bookmarks > Add Bookmarks from the menu.

Any of these actions opens a small dialogue box. Type a name for your bookmark (Safari pulls out the webpage's title automatically for you) and choose a destination, either the Bookmarks bar or the menu.

When you've finished, simply click the book icon on the Bookmarks bar to exit the Bookmarks area.

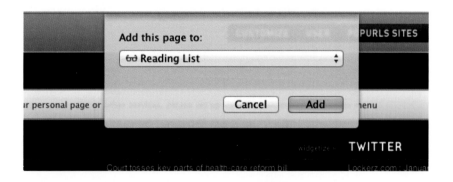

 **DID YOU KNOW?**

Most people organise their bookmarks in the Bookmarks menu, but sometimes you need a bookmark at your fingertips. If that's so, put your new bookmark in the Bookmarks bar.

 HOT TIP: You can also create bookmarks by dragging the little icon to the left of the webpage address directly to your Bookmarks bar.

Using bookmarks

Now that you've saved a few bookmarks, how do you use them? It's one thing to have access to the little handy reminders of your favourite sites, it's another thing to actually click on them.

Remember when I said you could save your bookmarks in the Bookmarks menu or the Bookmarks bar? Well, that choice you made about where to save a bookmark will determine how you use them.

1 If you saved a bookmark in the Bookmarks bar, click the right bookmark on the bar. Safari will immediately open the site referenced in that bookmark.

2 If you saved a bookmark in the Bookmarks menu, click the book icon to the far left on the Bookmarks bar, then click the bookmark you want in the list of bookmarks.

? DID YOU KNOW?

If you've got a lot of bookmarks, you can use the search function built into the bookmarks list to narrow your list with a search phrase.

Organising bookmarks

At some point you're going to be happily bookmarking favourite sites and other interesting content and realise that you've got way too many bookmarks. What was once a neat little list has become a monster!

Fortunately, it's very easy to organise your bookmarks using folders. These folders are similar to your file folders, except they work only with Safari bookmarks.

To organise your bookmarks:

1 Click the book icon on the far left of the Bookmarks bar.

2 Under Collections in the sidebar, click on the Bookmarks Menu icon.

3 To add a folder, click the + button at the bottom of the sidebar.

4 Give your folder a name.

5 Select and drag whichever bookmarks you want into your new folder.

DID YOU KNOW?

You can also drag files and folders on your Mac to your bookmarks in Safari. Safari will happily link to them.

Updating bookmarks

Every once in a while, you'll need to update your bookmarks. Either the name you gave a bookmark no longer makes sense, or the URL for a webpage has changed. Either way, you'll need to keep your bookmarks up to date.

To update a bookmark:

1 Click the book icon on the Bookmarks bar.

2 Click the Bookmarks menu collection in the sidebar.

3 Find the bookmark you want to change.

4 If you want to change the bookmark's name (for example, if it has a really strange or very long name), click the name once, then click again when it changes colour and give it a new name.

5 If you want to change the bookmark's URL (for example, if it has changed), click the address once, then click again when it changes colour and give it a new URL.

6 When you've finished, click the book icon again to return to browsing the Web.

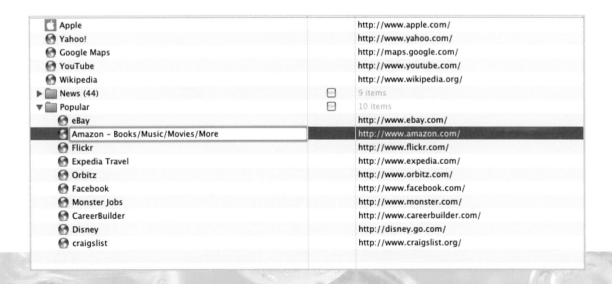

Exporting and importing bookmarks

Sometimes you end up with such a great list of bookmarks that you want to share it with friends. Or maybe you do a bit of research at home and want to have the same bookmarks on your Mac at work.

The tedious way to do this is to print out a list of all your bookmarks and then use that list to manually bookmark those same sites on another computer. Not only is that tedious, it's unnecessary, because Safari lets you export bookmarks.

To export your bookmarks in Safari:

1 Choose File > Export Bookmarks from the menu.

2 Choose a folder in which to save your bookmarks.

3 Click Save.

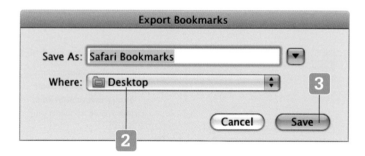

? DID YOU KNOW?

When you're ready to try something new, check out a website called Delicious (www.delicious.com). You can sign up for free and start saving your bookmarks on the Web. This is called 'social bookmarking' because you can then easily share your bookmarks with friends and colleagues. You can also access your bookmarks no matter what computer you're on!

Safari saves your bookmarks file as an HTML file. This file is not only easy to import, it can be viewed like any other webpage.

To import a bookmarks file:

1 Choose File > Import Bookmarks from the menu.

2 Browse to the appropriate bookmarks file and select it.

3 Click Import.

Deleting bookmarks

As you go along, you'll find yourself needing to cull your bookmarks. Sometimes you bookmark a site and use that bookmark for months at a time, then five years pass before you ever return to that site again. Or a website you've bookmarked shuts down or changes owners, and the content is either gone or you're not interested in what the new website owner has to offer.

Fortunately, Safari lets you delete bookmarks. To delete a bookmark:

1 Click the book icon on the Bookmarks bar.

2 Click the Bookmarks menu collection in the sidebar.

3 Find the bookmark you want to delete and click it once.

4 Press the delete button on your keyboard.

5 When you've finished, click the book icon to return to the Web.

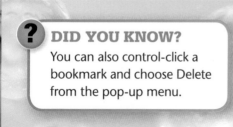

DID YOU KNOW?

You can also control-click a bookmark and choose Delete from the pop-up menu.

Saving a URL to your Desktop

Bookmarks aren't the only way to keep track of a favourite or informative website. You can also save links to a website directly to your Desktop (or any other folder in Finder).

To save a URL to your Desktop:

1 Click the icon next to a URL in the address field and hold down the button.

2 Drag the icon to your Desktop.

This will result in a new shortcut to that website added to your Desktop.

! ALERT: Be aware that sometimes you might get saved URLs from people who don't mean well. Their links might go to websites that are malicious in nature. Use common sense if you receive these kinds of shortcuts from others.

Using the history

Sometimes you forget to bookmark a favourite site. Days or weeks may go by and you'll struggle to remember where you found a certain bit of information. Don't fret too much, though, because Safari keeps a pretty good history of which websites you've visited.

There are three different ways to take advantage of Safari's history:

1 Click the back button on your browser. This works only if you've visited the site recently and haven't shut down Safari since then.

2 If you can remember a part of a website's URL or address, start typing it in the address bar. As soon as you do, Safari will provide you with a list of suggestions from the history.

3 Click History on the Safari menu. You'll see a list of the most recent places you've visited, plus a menu option to see all entries.

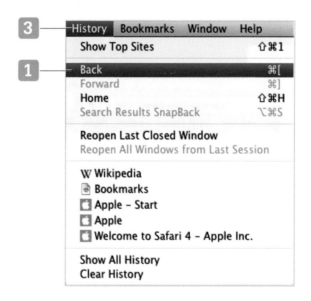

ALERT: If you're concerned about privacy, choose History > Clear History from the menu to clear out your browsing history.

Using tabs

Safari is a tabbed browser, which may not mean anything to you right now, but believe me, using tabs will make you a lot better organised.

In the old days of surfing the Web, if you wanted to visit more than one website at the same time, you had to open up a new window for each website. What you ended up with was a display full of windows. It wasn't very tidy and it took up a lot of real estate.

Because Safari is a modern web browser, it supports the concept of tabbed browsing. Instead of opening a new window to view a second website, you can simply open a new tab.

To open up a new tab:

● Press ⌘ T on the keyboard. This will create a new tab that you can now browse the web with. Simply click a bookmark or enter a URL in the address field to browse a website.

Sometimes you might want to purposefully open a new tab when you click a link, even though the link's behaviour is to open a new window or just refresh the window it's in.

To open a link as a new tab:

● Hold down the Command key (⌘) and then click the link. The new document opens in a new tab.

 HOT TIP: You can move any tab to a new window by choosing Window > Move Tab to New Window from the menu.

Making the fonts bigger or smaller on a webpage

If you're getting to the point where you need reading glasses (like me), or you're still young and spry but getting tired of reading the tiny little fonts that so many designers seem fond of, or you end up at a size with really huge letters that don't seem to fit on your screen, don't worry. Safari can help you adjust things for your comfort.

To make the fonts bigger on a webpage:

- Press ⌘ + on the keyboard.
- Alternatively, choose View > Make Text Bigger from the menu.

To make the fonts smaller on a webpage:

- Press ⌘ − on the keyboard.
- Alternatively, choose View > Make Text Smaller from the menu.

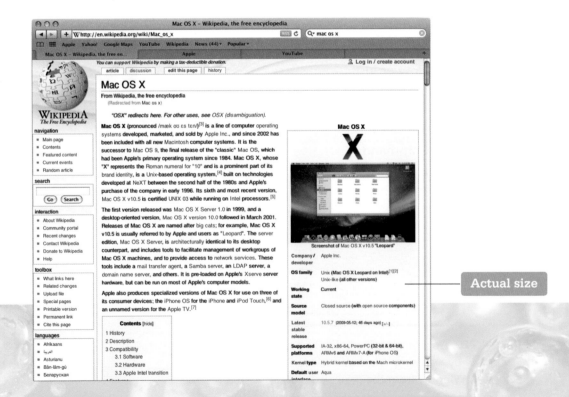

Bigger text

Smaller text

? DID YOU KNOW?

These commands only affect the text on a page. Safari won't change the size of images, nor will it try to change the general layout of a page.

Reloading a page

If you're reading a blog, a page generated by some kind of dynamic application, a shopping site or places like eBay or *The Times* of London's website, then often you might need to reload the page to get updates.

After all, something's probably changed on the site – there are new headlines, updated bids, better prices on inventory or a new blog post.

For these cases you'll need to reload the page. Safari lets you reload pages in a variety of ways:

1 Press ⌘ R on the keyboard.

2 Click the Reload button on the toolbar (it's next to the URL field).

3 Choose View > Reload Page from the menu.

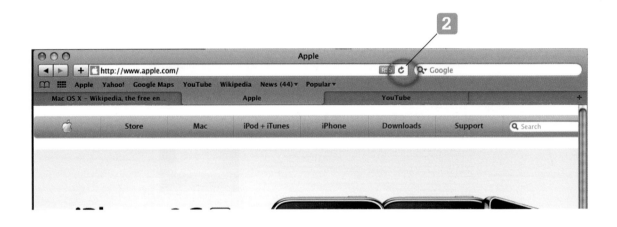

Printing a webpage

If you're like most people, sometimes you just need hard-copy proof of what you find on the Web. You might be doing some research for a project, or you just need to compare two different websites. Either way, sometimes websites shut down or go away, or the content on them changes. Printing webpages lets you create a paper trail.

To print a webpage, you can do **one** of the following:

1 Press ⌘ P on the keyboard.

2 Alternatively, choose File > Print from the menu.

Either of these opens up the Print dialogue, where you can choose a printer, set your colour options and even save the webpage as a PDF document.

? **DID YOU KNOW?**

If you'd rather save a webpage as a PDF, click the PDF button and choose Save As PDF from the menu.

Viewing the source code on a page

You might not do it often, but every once in a while (maybe out of curiosity or professional necessity) you'll need to have a look at the source code that makes a webpage work.

If you're not familiar with how websites work, each is written in a markup language known as HTML. HTML stands for HyperText Markup Language and its components allow web authors to create headlines, paragraphs, links and tables, and attach images and other elements to a webpage.

Normally, Safari hides all of this from you, but it's easy to see the markup, doing **one** of the following:

1 Choose View > View Source from the menu.

2 Alternatively, control-click on the webpage and choose View Source from the pop-up menu.

Once you do either of these, the webpage's HTML source code will appear in a second window for viewing.

Mailing webpage contents to another person

Sometimes you find yourself looking at something so interesting that you just need to email it to someone else. Safari makes this pretty easy, and in fact, you get two choices for sharing via email:

- You can send someone a link to the page you're looking at.
- You can send them the contents of the webpage embedded in the email.

To send someone a link, you can:

1 Choose File > Mail Link to this Page from the menu or press shift ⌘ I on the keyboard.

2 Compose an email to that person (don't forget their email address) and hit send.

To send someone the contents of a webpage directly in an email, you can:

3 Choose File > Mail Contents of this Page from the menu or press ⌘ I on the keyboard.

4 Compose an email to that person (don't forget their email address) and hit send.

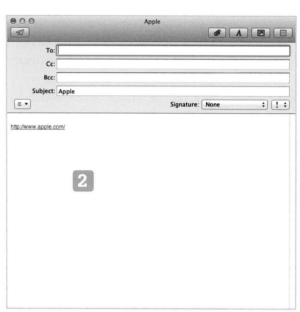

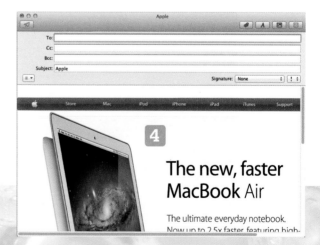

> **? DID YOU KNOW?**
>
> You could also highlight the URL, copy it with ⌘ C and then paste the URL into the message of an email.

Downloading files from the Web

Some days you'll need to download something from a website. You'll want to read a PDF, download a spreadsheet to see how it works, grab a music file or download some software for your Mac.

In most cases, downloading a file from the Web is as easy as clicking a link or image that points to that download. In other cases, however, you might want to download an image that's part of a website layout or photo gallery. To download that kind of file:

1 Control-click on the image and choose Save Image to 'Downloads' or Save Image As from the pop-up menu.

2 Confirm the name and destination of the downloaded file.

3 Click Save.

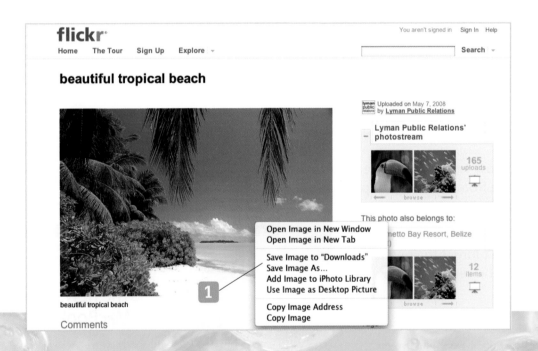

Blocking Web ads

Sometimes you end up on websites that are loaded down with ads. If you're like me, you find ads not only annoying (they blink, jump, bleep and shake too much for my comfort) but also tiresome. Just think of all the time and effort Safari has to put in just to show you all those ads!

Your Web surfing could use a bit of optimising. To block Web ads (and other types of content as well):

1 Choose Safari > Preferences from the menu (or press ⌘ , on the keyboard).

2 Click the Security tab.

3 In the Web content section, tick or untick any kind of content you want to block/unblock.

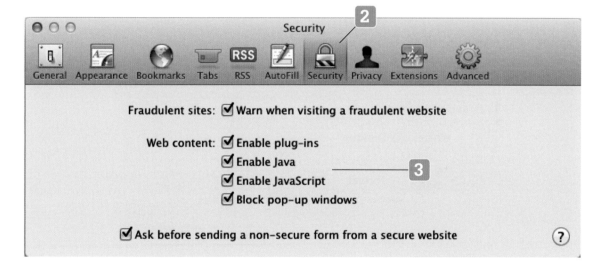

ALERT: It's a good idea to let Safari tell you if you're visiting a fraudulent site!

Saving a webpage to your Mac

Sometimes a bookmark or print-out just won't do – sometimes you need to have a copy of the actual page you visited. Yes, it might change in the near future, but you don't care. There's something about the layout, the way the images are aligned, how the text and graphics work together that speaks to you.

For whatever reason, you need to have a copy of a webpage for your records. To save a webpage to your Mac:

1 Choose File > Save As from the menu (or press ⌘ S on the keyboard).

2 Choose a location for your downloaded files.

3 If you want to view a working webpage, choose Web Archive as the download format.

4 If you want to view HTML source, choose Source as the download format.

5 Click Save.

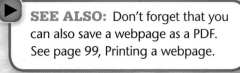

SEE ALSO: Don't forget that you can also save a webpage as a PDF. See page 99, Printing a webpage.

5 Contacts and events

Introduction

Besides organising files, reading and sending email and surfing the Web, you're probably going to be spending a great deal of your time keeping track of your friends, family and colleagues and also your calendar.

Your Mac comes with two pieces of free software that let you handle contacts and events: Address Book handles the people in your life and iCal handles all the places you have to be and things you have to do. Together, they make for an extremely impressive pair of tools.

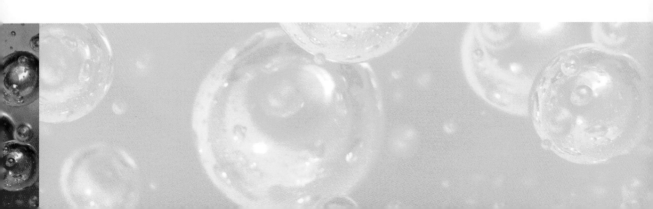

Starting Address Book

Address Book is a versatile application with one focus: to keep all the people in your life organised. You can create new contacts, store all kinds of information about them (such as their phone numbers, email addresses, snail mail addresses and so on), assign them to various groups, add photographs and write notes about them.

Before you can do any of these things, though, you have to start Address Book.

To start Address Book:

- Click the Address Book icon on the Dock.

When Address Book opens, you will see that it's broken up into three areas:

- A toolbar along the top with a few buttons and a search bar.
- A main window with three columns: Group, Name and then details about a selected contact.
- A footer with + buttons for adding groups and contacts and an edit button for the displayed contact.

Creating a new contact

Before you can do anything else with Address Book, you have to create a new contact. The easiest way to create a contact is to do **one** of the following:

1 Choose File > New Card from the menu.

2 Press ⌘ N on the keyboard.

3 Click the + button at the bottom of the Name column.

3

Once that's done, you'll see a blank contact on the screen.

- Enter a last name and first name.
- Enter a company name if appropriate.
- Enter any phone numbers you might have.
- Enter an email address if you have one.
- Enter any other information, such as a birthday or address.
- Click the Edit button on the footer when you've finished.

? DID YOU KNOW?

If you click the square icon in the lower left hand corner, you can change to a single contact view without having to see groups.

Editing a contact

People move to new homes, get new jobs and get new emails and phone numbers. Keeping your contacts list up to date is an important job, allowing you to stay in touch.

To edit a contact in Address Book:

1 Click a contact's name in the All Contacts column.

2 In the footer click the Edit button.

3 Make whatever updates you need to make.

4 Click the Edit button in the footer when you've finished.

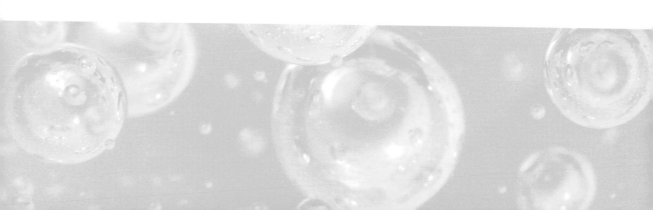

Deleting a contact

Sometimes you end up with a contact in your Address Book that you don't want to have. They may be a person whom you're no longer friendly with, or perhaps they were just someone you bumped into once (at a conference, for example) and don't ever speak to or otherwise communicate with.

Whatever the case may be, you need some way to delete contacts.

To delete a contact in Address Book:

1 Choose the contact's name in the All Contacts column.

2 Press the delete button on the keyboard.

3 Confirm your choice by clicking the Delete button on the confirmation pop-up.

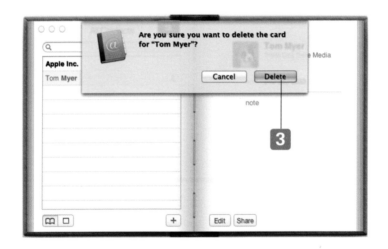

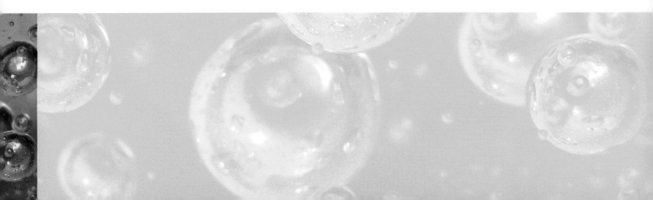

Adding a contact from an email

Adding contacts manually may seem like a good idea, but it would be nice to add people as you communicate with them – perhaps when you send and receive emails.

Thankfully, your Mail application knows how to work with Address Book. Here are three different ways you can add contact information to Address Book from Mail:

1 Click their email address in the From, To, Cc or Bcc fields and choose Add to Address Book from the menu.

2 Highlight any part of a message that looks like an address or phone number, control-click and choose either New Contact or Add to Existing.

3 Choose Window > Previous Recipients from the menu to see a list of previous recipients. Search or browse for contacts, select the ones you want and click Add to Address Book.

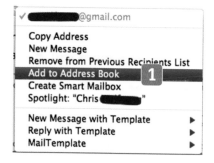

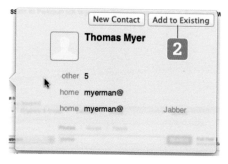

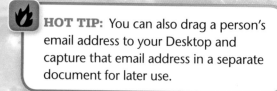

HOT TIP: You can also drag a person's email address to your Desktop and capture that email address in a separate document for later use.

Creating Address Book groups

Having a bunch of people in your Address Book is all well and good, but at some point you'll want to start organising your contacts into groups.

Address Book lets you organise your contacts into two types of groups:

- Regular groups, which consist of contacts that you manually organise.
- Smart groups, which share some kind of criteria (like a certain employer, postcode or some other characteristic).

To create a regular group, you can:

1 Choose File > New Group from the menu.

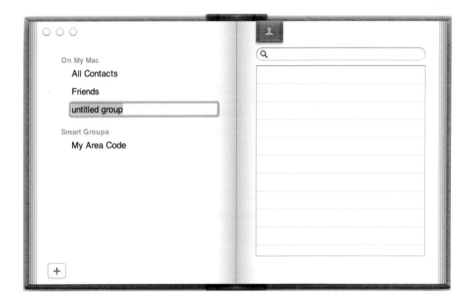

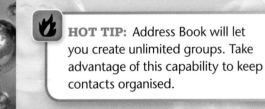

HOT TIP: Address Book will let you create unlimited groups. Take advantage of this capability to keep contacts organised.

Once you've created a group, give it a name. To assign contacts to a group, simply select them with your mouse and drag them to the group.

To create a smart group:

1 Choose File > New Smart Group from the menu.

2 Give your new smart group a suitable name.

3 Add criteria for the smart group by using the + button and entering criteria.

4 For example, to capture everyone with the same area code:

- Set the first dropdown to Phone.
- Set the second dropdown to begins with.
- Enter an area code.
- Click OK.

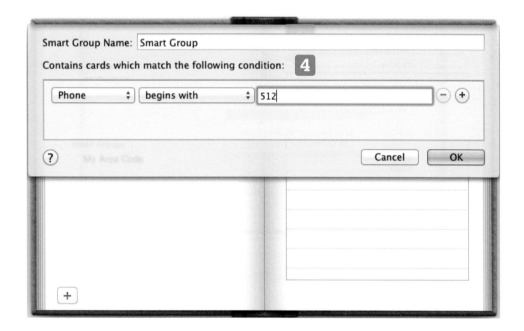

Sending an email to everyone in a group

If you've created any group, it's time to take advantage of an extremely handy feature in Address Book: sending an email to everyone in a group.

To send an email to everyone in a group:

1 Control-click a group name in the Group column.

2 Choose to send an email from the pop-up menu.

3 Mail opens a new message with all the email addresses from that group. Compose a message and click Send.

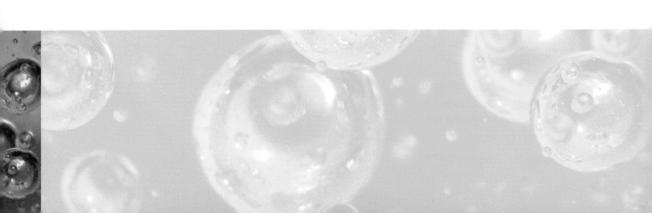

Merging contacts

If you're like most busy people, you might inadvertently end up with duplicate records for a contact. You might have work information in one contact record, personal information in another and yet other information in a third. This isn't unlikely in this age where people use different email addresses for different purposes.

However common this may be, it tends to make your contact list a bit untidy. To remedy the situation, Address Book offers an easy way to merge your contacts, saving you the time and effort it would take to do all of that manually.

To merge contacts:

1 Select the contacts you want to merge from the Name column.

2 Choose Card > Merge Selected Cards from the menu (or press ⌘ I on the keyboard).

Address Book quickly merges the selected contacts into a single contact.

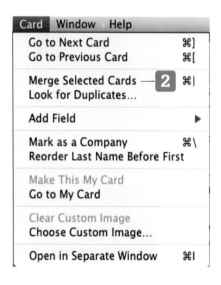

DID YOU KNOW?

You can get Address Book to look for duplicates by choosing Card > Look for Duplicates. It will find all instances of duplicate data and merge those contacts for you.

Searching contacts

If you've got a lot of contacts, you can only go so far with organisational skills. You'll only be able to remember a part of someone's name, or just their phone number, or some part of their email address. At some point you'll need to run some kind of search.

Like all other Mac applications, Address Book comes with a search bar. This search function can help you narrow down your contacts and allows you to find exactly who you're looking for.

To run a search:

1 Click inside the search bar.

2 Enter a search phrase. Remember that you can search for email addresses, phone numbers, names, addresses and other information.

3 As you type, the list of names changes to match the search phrase.

? **DID YOU KNOW?**

You can enter practically any data into the search field: postal codes, phone numbers, city names and so on. Address Book will try to match your contacts.

Set up your own contact info

What's the point of having a list of contacts if you don't have an entry for yourself? Fortunately, Address Book has a tiny bit of functionality that allows you to create a contact and designate it as your own contact information.

To create your own contact:

1 Choose File > New Card from the menu.

2 Press ⌘ N on the keyboard.

3 Click the + button at the bottom of the Name column.

Once that's done, you'll see a blank contact on the screen.

4 Enter whatever contact information you want, such as your name, email addresses and phone numbers.

5 Click the Edit button on the footer when you've finished.

6 Choose Card > Make this my Card from the menu.

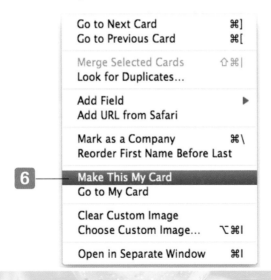

Starting iCal

iCal is a free calendar and events management tool that will help you stay on top of all your appointments and reminders. You can create all kinds of events, invite others to those events, make recurring events and do other useful things, such as organise your events into different calendars.

Before you can do any of that, you have to start up iCal.

To start iCal:

1 Click the iCal icon in the Dock (it should look like a calendar page with today's date on it).

When you first open iCal, you'll see that it's divided into three parts:

- A toolbar along the top with several buttons to switch views (Day, Week, Month and Year) and a search bar.
- A main view that shows your events in whatever format you've selected.
- A right sidebar that shows Reminders.

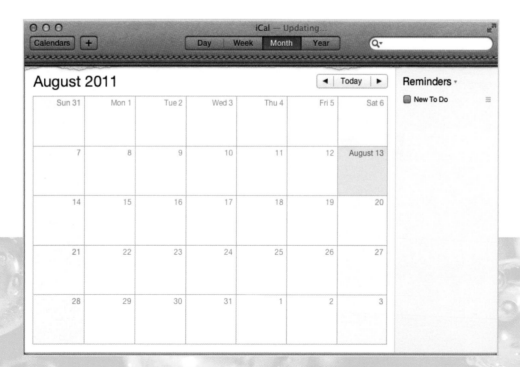

Creating a new event

Before doing anything else, let's create a new event together: your birthday.

1 Switch to month view by clicking the Month button on the toolbar.

2 Use the forward arrow to navigate to the month that contains your next birthday.

3 Double-click the day that represents your birthday. A New Event form pops up.

4 Click the title and enter 'My Birthday'.

5 Click the text next to location and jot down where your celebration will be held, if you know.

6 If your birthday is an all-day celebration (as it should be!) then tick the all-day tickbox.

7 Click Done.

Your new event appears in the calendar.

? DID YOU KNOW?
You can create recurring events too, but that's a topic I'll cover in a few pages!

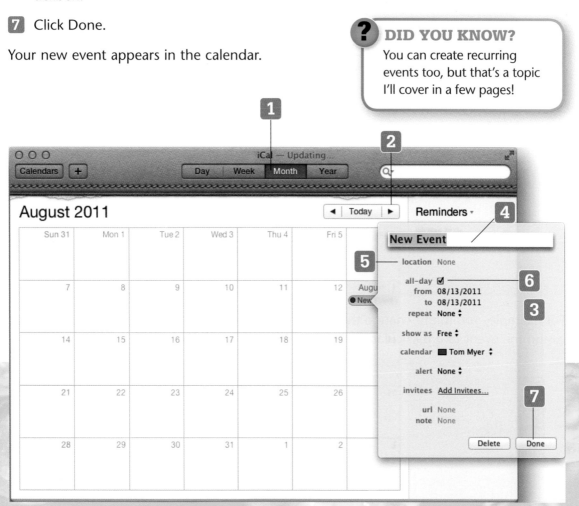

Updating an event

It happens all the time. An event gets delayed for a few days, or it changes location, or something else happens, and you find yourself needing to update its details.

Luckily, making updates is pretty painless in iCal.

To update an event:

1 Navigate to the event in iCal.

2 When you've found it, double-click the event to open it.

3 Click Edit.

4 Make whatever changes you need to and click Done.

For example, you might change the start or end time, add some notes, add an alarm or assign the event to a particular calendar (of which more later).

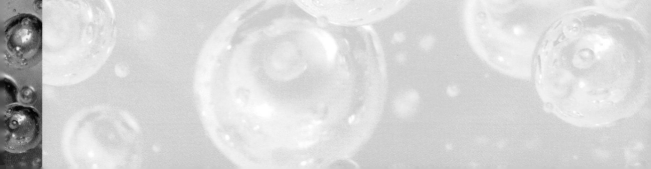

Deleting an event

Sometimes an event is cancelled or you no longer have an interest in actually attending it. You can leave it be, of course, but then you might become a little confused as to whether you actually went to the meeting or not.

In the short term, the easiest thing to do is to delete the event.

To delete an event:

1 Navigate to the event in iCal.

2 Click the event once.

3 Press the Delete key on the keyboard or choose Edit > Delete from the menu.

Undo	⌘Z
Redo	⇧⌘Z
Cut	⌘X
Copy	⌘C
Paste	⌘V
Delete	
Select All	⌘A
Duplicate	⌘D
Show Event	
Edit Event...	⌘E
Get Info	⌘I
Show Inspector	⌥⌘I
Find	⌘F
Show Spelling and Grammar	⇧⌘:
Special Characters...	

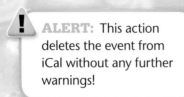

ALERT: This action deletes the event from iCal without any further warnings!

Creating calendars in iCal

iCal uses the concept of calendars to help you organise events. When you first start out, all your events go into a default calendar, but as you continue to use the tool, you might realise that you need different kinds of calendars.

For example, you might have one calendar for your business events, another one for school events and yet another for your college classes. I've seen colleagues use different calendars to organise the different types of meetings they have: in person, conference call and webinars.

Each calendar has a different colour, which makes different kinds of events easy to distinguish on the iCal display.

To create a new calendar in iCal:

1 Choose File > New Calendar from the menu.

2 When the new calendar shows up in the sidebar, give it a new name.

New Event	⌘N
New Reminder	⌘K
New Calendar	▶
New Calendar Group	⇧⌘N
Import	▶
Export	▶
Close	⌘W
Print...	⌘P

? DID YOU KNOW?

The new calendar name will appear in the Calendar dropdown available to you when you create a new event. Simply choose it from the dropdown to assign it to an event.

Creating a recurring event

Some events, like your birthday, staff meetings and others hopefully more fun than staff meetings, often happen over and over again. Instead of creating individual events, it's much smarter to create a recurring event.

To create a recurring event:

1 Create a new event by double-clicking in a particular day on the calendar view.

2 Enter a title, location, date and time for your new event.

3 Next to repeat, click the dropdown and choose how often you want to repeat. You can have events that repeat daily, weekly, monthly, yearly or some other custom arrangement (like every other month or twice a week).

4 Next to end, make a selection from the dropdown. You can choose Never, After (which allows you to set a certain number of repeats), or a particular date.

5 Make any other edits you need and click Done when you've finished.

 HOT TIP: If you don't like the colour assigned to a calendar, simply control-click the calendar name and choose Get Info from the pop-up menu. Change the colour and any other details in the dialogue box.

Inviting someone to an event

Sometimes you'll find yourself creating an event that requires somebody else to attend. You might be organising an outing of friends to the theatre, putting together a business meeting or workshop, or planning a family reunion.

In any case, you can take advantage of iCal's invitation process.

To invite someone to attend an event:

1 Create an event by double-clicking a day in the calendar view.

2 Enter the details of your event, such as its title, location, day and time.

3 Next to attendees, click Add Attendees.

4 In the text field that appears, start entering names from your contact list in Address Book, or email addresses if they're not in Address Book. Separate your list of names with commas.

5 Finish adding other details to your event, then click Done when you've finished.

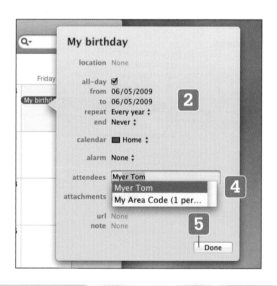

Changing your iCal view

On some days, you want to get the big picture of your busy schedule: you want to see an entire month at a time. On other days, you just want to know what lies in the week ahead. Sometimes you're happy to just keep up with a single day's incredibly packed schedule.

Once again, iCal comes to the rescue, providing you with a simple way to change your view of events (literally).

1 To see just one day's worth of events, click the Day button in the toolbar.

2 To see a week's worth of events at a time, click the Week button in the toolbar.

3 To see a month's worth of events at a time, click the Month button in the toolbar.

4 To see a year's worth of events at a time, click the Year button in the toolbar.

Seeing today's events

If you've been wandering around iCal for a while, trying to figure out what your schedule might look like three months from now, or you were doing research into what you were doing three months ago, you can get a bit lost. Getting back to today's date might be a bit too tedious if you're just navigating with the arrow buttons on the toolbar.

Well, iCal won't let you become overwhelmed with boredom, I assure you. If you need to get back to the current day, do **any** of the following:

1 Click the Today button on the toolbar.

2 Choose View > Go To Today from the menu.

3 Press ⌘ T on the keyboard.

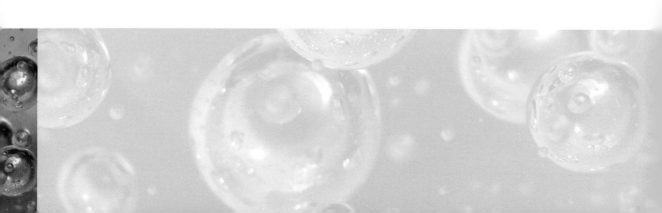

Searching for an event

No matter how well organised you are, or how good your memory is, eventually you're going to be looking for an event and no amount of back and forth navigation will help you find it. You'll remember that the event was at a certain location or on a certain day, but not much else.

Like other Mac applications, iCal comes with a powerful search function that lets you quickly find the events you're looking for.

To run a search:

1 Click inside the search bar.

2 Enter a search phrase. Remember that you can search for event titles, locations, start times, notes and other data.

3 You can limit what you search by clicking the down arrow next to the magnifying glass and choosing an option (such as event titles only or locations only).

4 As you type, the list of events in the search list changes to match the search phrase.

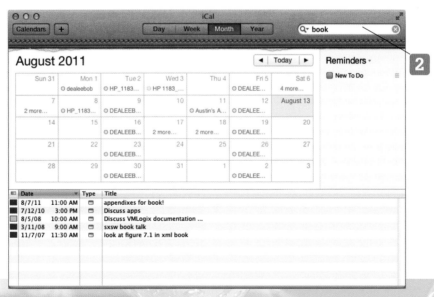

6 Photos

Introduction

Some of your most important memories will be captured as photographs. Most people have made the switch to digital photography and you probably have a whole bunch of digital images of birthday parties, holidays, good times with friends and family, weddings and much more.

One of the things that your Mac is exceptionally good at is helping you keep track of images, music and movies. The application that you'll be using to keep track of images is iPhoto, an easy and intuitive tool that lets you import photos, organise them, edit them, rate them and share them with others.

Another application I'll be covering very briefly is a fun one: it's called Photo Booth. It allows you to take photos of yourself using your Mac's built-in iSight camera.

Starting iPhoto

Before you can start working with photographs, you have to start iPhoto.

To start iPhoto:

- Click the iPhoto icon on the Dock. (It looks like a camera superimposed on a beach sunrise photo.)

When you open iPhoto for the first time, this is what you'll see:

1 A sidebar (also known as the Source list) that contains a list of events. Events are made up of individual times that you've imported images from a camera.

2 Along with events, the sidebar can contain albums that you create. You might have an album for a holiday or an album that contains photos of your pets. You can also create smart albums and slideshows.

3 The main window, next to the sidebar, is where you'll work with your photos.

4 A footer with various functional buttons that allow you to create albums, smart albums and slideshows, show information on a photo, find photos by date or keyword, view photos in full-screen mode, run searches and adjust the size of thumbnail images in the viewer.

? DID YOU KNOW?

A roll can consist of one photo or hundreds of them, or anything in between. It just depends on how often you update iPhoto.

🔥 HOT TIP: You can create albums and slideshows that contain images from many different events.

Importing photos from a camera or iPhone

If you own a digital camera or iPhone, transferring photos from that device and into iPhoto is pretty easy. Here's what you do:

1 Connect your camera to your Mac with a USB cable.

2 Make sure that you turn the camera on and set it to whatever mode it requires for viewing photos. Please read your camera's manual for more information.

3 As soon as your camera is connected, iPhoto switches to Import view and your camera appears in the Source list in the sidebar.

4 You should also see a thumbnail preview of all the images you're about to import.

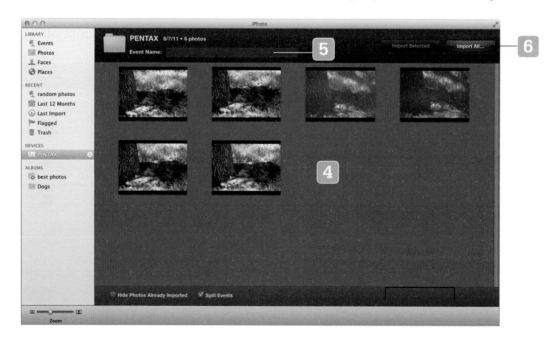

 **ALERT:** The best way to disconnect a camera is to click the Eject button next to the camera in the Source list.

5 Enter a name for the roll of pictures you're going to import, along with a description (this part is optional).

6 Click Import Selected or Import All.

If you want to delete photos from the camera after you've imported images, click the Delete Photos button in the dialogue box.

ALERT: Don't disconnect your camera until the import process finishes.

? DID YOU KNOW?
You can stop the import of photos at any time by clicking Stop Import.

Importing photos from a CD or other location

You're not just limited to importing photos from a camera, you can also import photos from the following sources:

- Images saved on a CD or DVD.
- Images saved on a Flash drive.
- Images saved on a folder on your Mac or other device.
- Images stored on a memory card (but you'll need a reader).

To import images from a CD, DVD, Flash drive or folder:

1 Choose File > Import to Library from the menu.

2 Navigate to where your images are stored.

3 When you've found the right folder, click Import.

Previewing photos

Now that you've imported some images from your camera, it's time to learn how to use the preview features in iPhoto.

Previewing a set of photos is very easy in iPhoto:

1 In the main viewing pane, click Events, then double-click the name of a roll.

2 When you do that, your photos will appear as a grid of thumbnails.

3 You can double-click one or more thumbnails to get a more detailed look at your photos.

4 You can control how many thumbnails you see in a row by adjusting the slider in the lower left part of the footer.

? DID YOU KNOW?

Once you select a roll, iPhoto will display a set of buttons that lets you edit those images, send them via email or create a slide show.

Viewing photos by date

Sometimes viewing your images by roll isn't that easy. You might end up with a lot of different rolls, or you may have too many images to deal with. Fortunately, iPhoto automatically categorises each roll by when you imported it into iPhoto.

What this means for you is that browsing by a year or month is very easy.

To browse by year:

1 In the Sources list in the sidebar, you should see one or more icons under Recent.

2 Click Last 12 Months to see your most recent photos.

3 If you've been taking photos for a while, you'll see a list of calendar years, each of which will let you see photos uploaded during that year.

Creating a slide show of photos

In a slide show, a series of photos appears sequentially, one after another. With iPhoto, you can create slide shows with any number of photos in them, in any order you wish.

What's even better is that once you create a slide show, it appears in the Source list alongside your photo albums and film rolls.

To create a slide show:

1 Either choose an entire roll from the Photos list or pick and choose individual photos.

2 Click the Slideshow button. It's in the footer and looks like an arrow.

3 iPhoto will change its screen to show you the slide show.

4 Pick a transition type from the Transition tab. You can add special effects, like transitions and the Ken Burns effect.

5 Add music to your slide show by clicking Music and choosing a song from iTunes.

6 Click Play when you're ready to view your slide show.

WHAT DOES THIS MEAN?

The 'Ken Burns' effect: This refers to a technique pioneered by documentary film maker Ken Burns – he panned and zoomed across still photographs to provide visual interest and drama.

Editing photos

iPhoto isn't just a great tool for organising your photographs and creating slide shows, it also has a set of editing tools that allows you to adjust brightness and contrast, remove red eye, retouch elements and more.

To edit a photo:

1 Select one or more thumbnails and click Edit.

2 To automatically darken or lighten an image to where it should be, click Enhance. You'll notice that overly exposed images get more contrast and underexposed photos get more brightness and detail.

3 You can also adjust contrast, brightness and other elements individually by clicking Adjust.

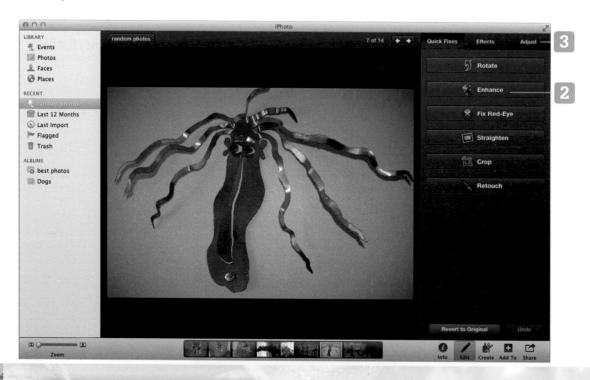

? DID YOU KNOW?

Once you edit an image it's easy to go back to its original form. Simply click Effects and then select the original version of the image.

4 Remove red eye in your photos with the Fix Red-Eye button.

5 Apply effects (like Black & White or Sepia Tones) by clicking Effects.

6 If you want to back out without making changes to your image(s), simply press the Escape key.

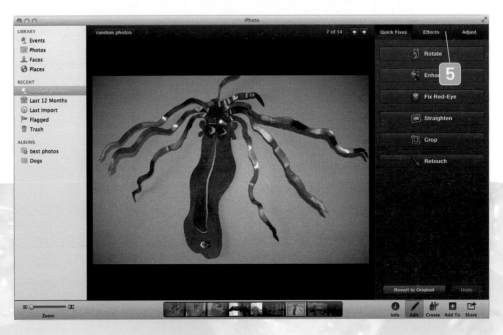

Cropping photos

Sometimes you end up with images that are just too big, or only have interesting portions surrounded by distracting or boring backgrounds. And sometimes you just want to cut someone out of your photos because he or she stood you up on one too many dates!

To crop a photo:

1 Select one thumbnail and click Edit.

2 Click Crop.

3 iPhoto places a crop rectangle over your image as a suggestion.

4 You can move this rectangle up and down or left and right as you need to.

5 You can also resize the crop rectangle by dragging any of the corners or dragging any of the sides to narrow or flatten the rectangle.

6 When you're happy with the crop, click Done.

7 You can always cancel out by pressing the Escape key.

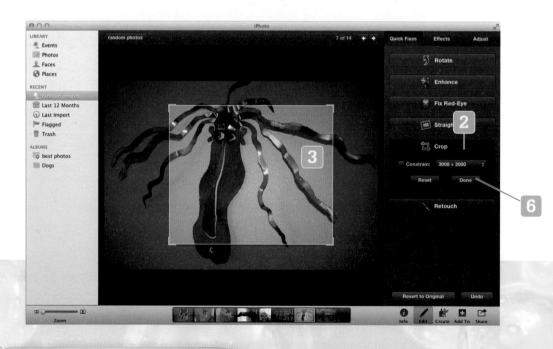

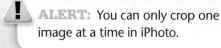

ALERT: You can only crop one image at a time in iPhoto.

Resizing photos

If you're working with a high-megapixel digital camera, a lot of times you end up with a really large image. For example, my Pentax 10-megapixel digital SLR shoots images that are 3000 pixels wide and almost as high, which means that they're hard to share or print.

iPhoto comes to the rescue once more, allowing you to resize images.

To resize an image:

1 Select one or more thumbnails and click Edit.

2 Click Crop.

3 Right above the word Constrain there's a dropdown with various size selections.

4 Change your image's size by making a selection. For example, you can constrain your image to 8 × 10, 4 × 6 (Postcard) or even landscape mode.

5 When you're happy with the resize, click Done.

6 You can always cancel out by pressing the Escape key.

Rotating photos

If you're like most people, then you've probably taken quite a few portrait shots that should have been landscape and vice versa. Sometimes this was just because you wanted to get the shot before something changed, other times you may not have realised you were holding the camera 'wrong'.

Not to worry, because iPhoto lets you rotate photos.

To rotate a photo:

1 Double-click one of the thumbnails.

2 Click Edit, then click Rotate.

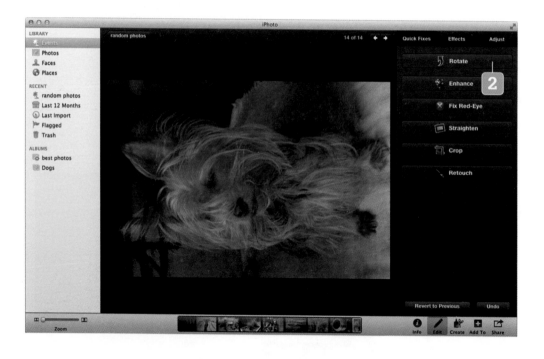

3 Each time you click Rotate, iPhoto will rotate your image 90 degrees, so you may need to click it several times in order to get the image where you want it.

> ## WHAT DOES THIS MEAN?
>
> **Portrait:** A vertical orientation on a photograph, such as when you take a portrait of a person or tall building.
>
> **Landscape:** A horizontal orientation of a photograph, such as when you take a photo of scenery.

Organising your photos into albums

In iPhoto, rolls give you a quick way to view your photos in basically the same groupings that you took the shots. You might have taken your camera on a trip, or taken a week's worth of shots that include a birthday party, some photos of your garden, maybe a few more of your new puppy, and then a sunset or two.

The end result of all these rolls is that sometimes you end up with photos scattered hither and yon that might otherwise belong together. To solve that little conundrum, iPhoto allows you to create an album. An album is any collection of photos that you think should go together, for example:

- All the photos related to a single holiday.
- All photos that you've taken on a beach.
- All photos of dogs.
- All photos of your son or daughter as they grow up over the years.

To create a photo album:

1 Click the Add To button in the footer.

2 Choose Album from the dropdown.

3 Give your album a name.

4 Click Create.

Once your album is created, it appears in the sidebar after your rolls. To add photos to an album, simply select one or more thumbnails and drag them to the album.

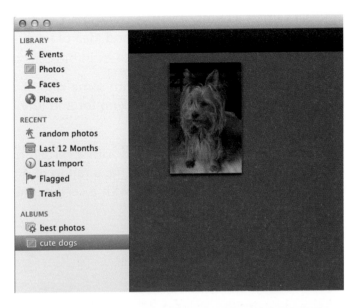

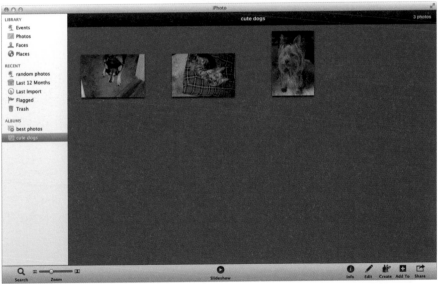

? DID YOU KNOW?

Adding photos to an album in no way removes them from their original rolls.

Creating smart albums

iPhoto allows you to create smart albums. If you've used smart folders in Finder or smart mailboxes in Mail, then you've got a pretty good idea of what smart albums will be like in iPhoto.

Essentially, a smart album is one that is populated with some kind of query. When you build a smart album, you tell iPhoto what you're looking for and it finds all the photos in its collections that meet those requirements.

For example, you may want to see only those photos with a certain rating, or with comments already applied, or a combination of criteria: a rating of 4 or higher, with comments, with a certain keyword in the filename, with a certain shutter speed.

To create a smart album:

1 Choose File > New > Smart Album from the menu.

2 Choose Smart Album from the dropdown.

3 Give your album a name.

4 Click Create.

5 Enter one or more criteria by using the dropdown.

6 Add criteria by clicking the + button.

7 Click OK when you've finished.

Tagging faces

Not only can you organise your photos by album, you can also tag people's faces in photographs and then have a record of your favourite people. Now, when you want to look at all the photos of your spouse, best friend, or grandchildren, you can do it quickly and easily.

To get started with Faces:

1 Click Faces in the left navigation bar.

2 iPhoto will show you three images with what it thinks are faces. To tag a face, write the name of the person in the box underneath the image.

3 You can continue adding faces to photos by clicking Show More Faces.

4 You can finish whenever you want by clicking Continue To Faces.

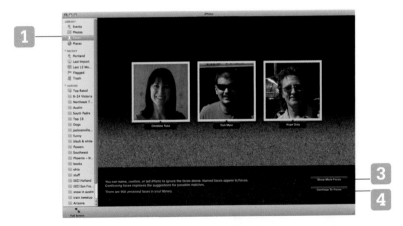

Once you're done, iPhoto will show you a list of names. Depending on how well you've trained iPhoto, you should see plenty of pictures for each person in a group of Faces!

Using Places

The Places feature in iPhoto lets you organise your pictures by where you took them. This is a convenient way to organise your pictures, especially if you do a lot of travelling. Think how easy it will be to show off those pictures of your last trip to Holland!

To get started with Places:

1 Select any event in the left navigation bar.

2 Click the Info button.

3 Start typing in a city and province or state. The name of the location should come up in a Google Search. Click the appropriate name.

4 Once you've selected a location, iPhoto should insert a map. Move the pin around to pinpoint the exact location.

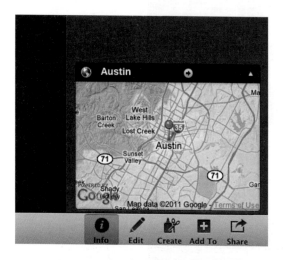

ALERT: You have to be connected to the Internet in order for Places to work.

Getting info on photos

At certain times, you'll need to know something about your photos: width and height, filename, exposure characteristics (like shutter speed and f-stop) and other information.

To get info on a photo:

1 Select a thumbnail.

2 Choose View > Info from the menu.

3 Image size information is listed in the upper right corner, for example 3000 × 2000 3.4 MB.

4 The camera's exposure settings are right below that, for example ISO 3200 f/5.6 1/60 (ISO, aperture, shutter speed).

5 The camera's make and model is on the top line, for example Pentax K100D.

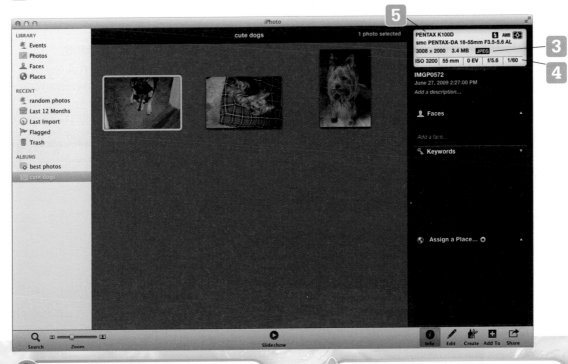

DID YOU KNOW?

If your camera supports EXIF information, then it will add all kinds of metadata to each picture, such as f-stop, shutter speed, focal length of the lens, flash exposure and more.

ALERT: You can only get information on one image at a time.

Adding keywords and comments to photos

Comments and keywords are bits of information you can add to your photos to make them easier to find and/or help you identify someone in a photo.

Using comments, you can add all kinds of information. Maybe you want to list all the people in the photo. Or perhaps you feel the need to capture information about exposure settings – f-stops and shutter speed, ISO speed and the like. Or maybe you just feel the need to write a haiku about each photo.

To add a comment to a photo:

1 Double-click an image.

2 Click the Info button in the footer.

3 Click the description and enter your notes.

Keywords, meanwhile, are labels you can add to help you find your photos later. For example, a certain photograph might feature your pet Yorkshire Terrier in a wheelbarrow. You could add various keywords to this photo: dog, yorkie, wheelbarrow, gardening and so on.

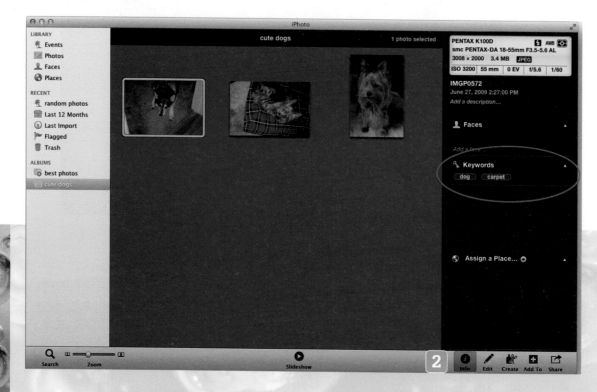

To add a keyword to a photo:

4 Select one or more thumbnails.

5 Choose Window > Show Keywords from the menu.

6 Drag whatever keywords you want from the bottom pane into the top pane.

7 Close the keyword window when you've finished.

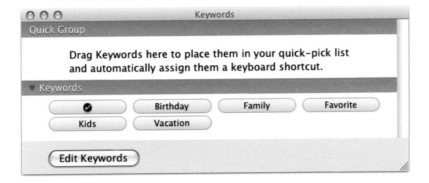

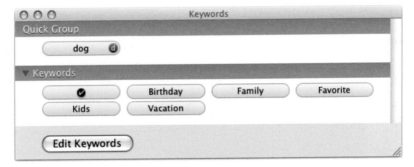

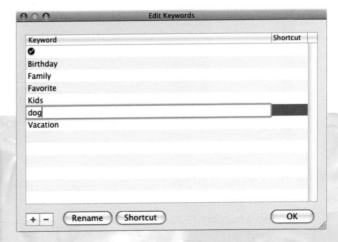

? DID YOU KNOW?

If you want to change the available keywords in the list, you can click Edit Keywords from this same window.

Rating photos

Let's face it, if you're like me, then most of the photos in your collection will be so so, but there will be a small handful that will just knock you out with their beauty, presentation or subject matter. And then there will be a whole bunch of photos in between.

iPhoto allows you to rate any photo to indicate how much you like it. You can then use these ratings to help organise your photo albums and to sort your collections.

To rate a photo:

1 Select one or more thumbnails.

2 Choose Photos > My Rating from the menu.

3 Choose how many stars (from 0 to 5) to assign to the selected images.

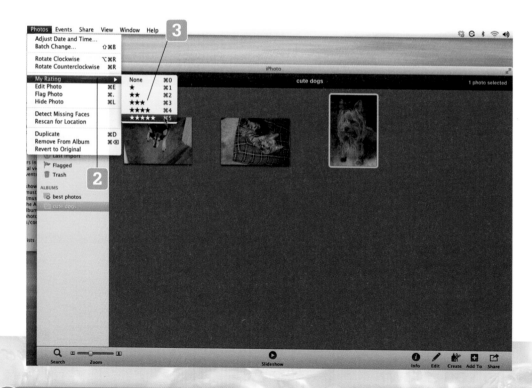

? DID YOU KNOW?

You can also rate a photo by pressing ⌘ and a number (1 to 5) while it is selected.

 HOT TIP: You can always change a rating by choosing a different number and remove a rating by selecting 0 stars.

Sorting photos

iPhoto normally displays your photos in the order that you imported them – in other words, by roll. However, you don't have to keep this sort order. You can order your photos by album, date, keyword, rating, title or even manually.

To change the sort order:

1 Choose View > Sort Photos from the menu.

2 Choose one of the following options:

- By Date. This arranges photos by the date you took them.
- By Keyword. This arranges photos alphabetically by their keywords.
- By Title. This arranges photos alphabetically by their titles.
- By Rating. This arranges photos from highest to lowest rating.
- Manually. This lets you drag photos into any order you like.

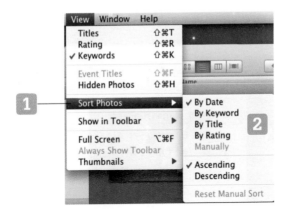

Emailing photos

What's the point of having a bunch of photos if you can't easily share them with someone else? That's just no fun at all.

iPhoto allows you to email one or more images to someone else. The images are sent as attachments to the recipient.

To email photos:

1 Select one or more thumbnails.

2 Choose Share > Email from the menu or click the Email icon in the toolbar.

3 Choose a size in pixels for your emailed photos from the Size dropdown menu.

4 Click Compose Message to open a new email in Mail.

Once your new email message is open, compose an email as you would normally. Notice that your images are attached to the email message.

DID YOU KNOW?
You can also click the Share button in the footer and choose Email.

Printing photos

Sometimes you don't just want your photos on your computer, you want them on your wall or in a physical photo album.

iPhoto, happily enough, allows you to print both single photos and contact sheets of photos (if you select more than one at the same time). To ensure quality, make sure that you're printing to a photo printer and that you have the right paper and enough quality ink.

To print your own photos:

1 Select one or more thumbnails.

2 Choose File > Print from the menu.

3 You can change your zoom and crop options using the Margins slider.

4 Click Print when you're ready to go.

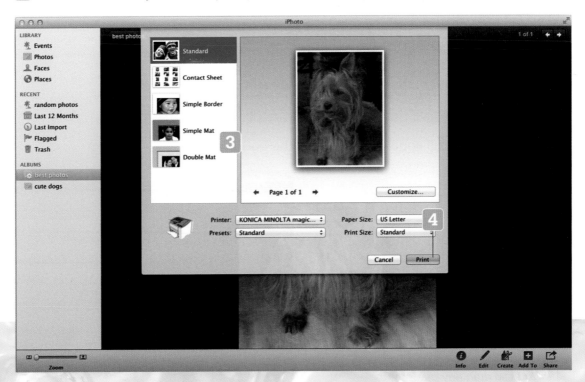

Taking a snapshot with Photo Booth

Have you ever been to a railway station or a supermarket and seen one of those photo booths with the curtains? Have you ever been inside with a friend and taken some goofy pictures together? The kind that run all in a sequence?

Well, Photo Booth on the Mac is like that, except it takes a picture of you with the built-in iSight camera. You can fire up Photo Booth and take funny or serious portraits of yourself or your friends, apply all kinds of effects (like black and white or an Andy Warhol-type effect) and then use the resulting image however you like – you can use it as your online avatar on social media sites or forums, or you can make it your official Address Book image.

To take a snapshot of yourself with Photo Booth:

1. Start Photo Booth by going to Applications and double-clicking the Photo Booth icon.

2. Select the type of snapshot you want to take: single shot, four-up or video.

3. Choose an effect by clicking the Effects button.

4. Click the snapshot button (it looks like a camera) when you're ready.

5. Photo Booth will give you a countdown and then take the snapshot.

Your new snapshot will appear in the roll at the bottom.

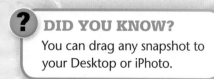

? DID YOU KNOW?
You can drag any snapshot to your Desktop or iPhoto.

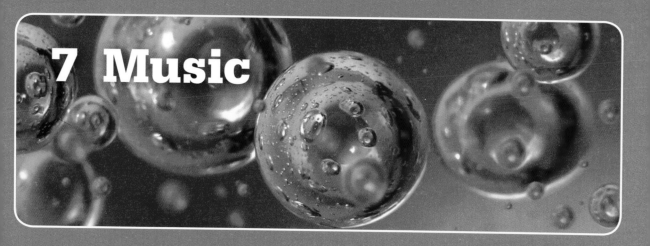

7 Music

Introduction

Much like your photos, your music collection says a lot about you. Do you stick to one genre of music, a particular artist or period, or do you have a more eclectic collection? If you're anything like me, you've got some classical, blues, rock, country and so-called 'world' music. Yes, you might have a favourite artist, but that probably doesn't keep you from exploring other options.

Your Mac comes with a great way to organise and enjoy your digital music – it's called iTunes. With iTunes, you can buy songs from the iTunes Store, import songs from your CD collection, play songs, organise them into different playlists, export songs to an iPod or iPhone, and rate your collection.

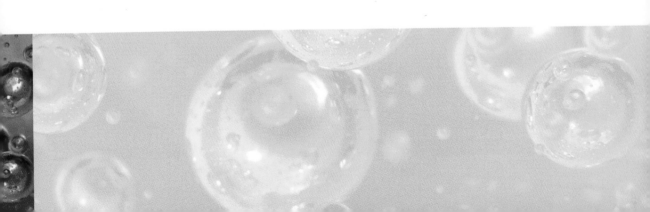

Starting iTunes

Before you can enjoy your music, you have to start up iTunes.

To start iTunes:

● Click the iTunes icon in the Dock (it looks like a CD with a musical note on it).

The iTunes interface is split into four parts:

1 A toolbar that runs along the top contains buttons that allow you to play and pause music, skip to the next or previous songs, control the volume, change your view of songs and albums, and run searches.

2 The sidebar contains links to your library of music, the iTunes Store, any devices you may have hooked up, and your playlists.

3 The main viewing area shows icons of albums or listings of songs, depending on where you are.

4 A footer that runs along the bottom contains various buttons that allow you to shuffle playlists, loop a playlist or song, and activate the Genius, among other things.

Buying a song from the iTunes Store

The first thing you're going to do is learn how to use the iTunes Store. Although you probably have a very large collection of CDs for importing songs, it's a good thing to get acquainted with the Store early on.

To buy a song from the iTunes Store:

1 In the sidebar, click iTunes Store. It's under the Store heading.

2 iTunes will access the Store and then present you with a view that displays the different types of music, video, movies, TV shows, audiobooks, podcasts and more that are available.

3 In the upper right-hand corner, run a search for your favourite artist.

4 The iTunes Store will display a set of results that match that artist. To buy a particular song, click the Buy Song button next to a song.

If there's money in your account, iTunes will deduct the amount from your balance and download the song. If you don't have a positive account balance, you'll be prompted to pay with a credit card or Paypal.

> **!** **ALERT:** You must have an iTunes account to access the Store. Don't worry, it's free and iTunes will prompt you to create an account if you don't have one.

Importing a song from a CD

If you're anything like me and most of my friends, you've probably got a CD collection that requires its own special room (or at least its own closet). And like me, you're probably passionate about your music, following artists' careers and musical genres.

One of the first things you'll want to do is start importing songs trapped on those CDs and get them into iTunes.

To import a CD:

1 Insert a music CD into your Mac's optical drive.

2 iTunes will display a list of songs from the CD in a window. All the songs will be ticked.

3 Deselect any songs you don't want to import.

4 Click the Import CD button, which is at the bottom of the iTunes window.

5 When the songs have finished importing, click the Eject symbol to the right of the CD.

Your new songs will appear in the Music library.

Playing songs

Playing songs is what iTunes is for, so let's start playing some and enjoying the music.

To play a song:

1 Click Music in the sidebar.

2 Click the song you want to hear from the list.

3 Click the play button in the toolbar or choose Controls > Play from the menu.

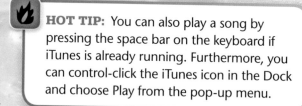

HOT TIP: You can also play a song by pressing the space bar on the keyboard if iTunes is already running. Furthermore, you can control-click the iTunes icon in the Dock and choose Play from the pop-up menu.

Pausing a song

If you're playing a song and you suddenly get a visitor or a phone call, it's only courteous to hit the pause button so you can listen to what the other person is saying. Later, you can continue to enjoy your music right where you left off.

To pause a song, you can do **any** of the following:

1 Click the Pause button in the toolbar.

2 Choose Controls > Pause from the menu.

3 Press the space bar on the keyboard.

4 Control-click the iTunes icon in the Dock and choose Pause from the pop-up menu.

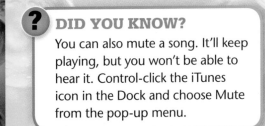

? DID YOU KNOW?

You can also mute a song. It'll keep playing, but you won't be able to hear it. Control-click the iTunes icon in the Dock and choose Mute from the pop-up menu.

Skipping to the previous or next song

There will be times when you're listening to a song and you'll want to skip to some other song. Or a song will end and you'll want to hear it again.

iTunes gives you all sorts of ways to move to different songs. You could, for example, simply choose another song in the list and play that. But sometimes the easiest way to navigate is to use the Next and Previous buttons.

To navigate to the next song, you can do **one** of the following:

1 Click the Next button in the toolbar (it looks like two arrows pointing to the right).

2 Choose Controls > Next from the menu.

3 Control-click the iTunes icon in the Dock and choose Next from the pop-up menu.

To navigate to the previous song, you can do **one** of the following:

4 Click the Previous button in the toolbar (it looks like two arrows pointing to the left).

5 Choose Controls > Previous from the menu.

6 Control-click the iTunes icon in the Dock and choose Previous from the pop-up menu.

Creating playlists

Having all your songs in one giant library called Music will only serve you for a little while. At some point you'll purchase or import so many songs that there will be no way to keep things properly organised.

iTunes comes to the rescue with its playlist feature. A playlist can be any list of songs. It can be organised by artist, year, genre or even other groupings that make sense to you: songs that make you sad, songs that remind you of summer, songs with heinous use of trumpets, or songs that make you want to dance.

It doesn't matter, because playlists are all about you and your tastes. You can create playlists and then drag songs into those playlists. Then, when you're ready to enjoy a playlist, you can click that playlist in the sidebar and play the songs in it.

To create a playlist:

1 Click the + button in the footer.

2 Give your new playlist a name.

3 Select one or more songs from the Music library and drag them onto your playlist name in the sidebar.

Sorting songs

Whether you're looking at your Music library or one of your playlists, songs are listed with column headers along the top. You might have column headers for song name, song duration, artist name, album name and other information.

Like with other applications on the Mac, such as Finder and Mail, each column header allows you to sort the list by the contents. Click once and you sort ascending (A–Z), click again and it toggles to descending sort (Z–A).

▶	Name	Time ▼	Artist	Album	Genre	Rating
1	☑ Hot Rod	8:31	Royal Crown Revue	Caught In The Act	Jazz	
2	☑ Hey Pachuco	8:30	Royal Crown Revue	Caught In The Act	Jazz	
3	☑ Poppity Pop Goes The Motorcy...	7:00	Royal Crown Revue	Caught In The Act	Jazz	
4	☑ Boogie After Midnight	4:51	Royal Crown Revue	Caught In The Act	Jazz	
5	☑ Honey Child	3:49	Royal Crown Revue	Caught In The Act	Jazz	
6	☑ The Mooch	3:48	Royal Crown Revue	Caught In The Act	Jazz	
7	☑ Park's Place	3:19	Royal Crown Revue	Caught In The Act	Jazz	
8	☑ Who Dat?	3:11	Royal Crown Revue	Caught In The Act	Jazz	
9	☑ Barflies At The Beach	3:01	Royal Crown Revue	Caught In The Act	Jazz	
10	☑ Something's Gotta Give	2:45	Royal Crown Revue	Caught In The Act	Jazz	
11	☑ Mousetrap	2:38	Royal Crown Revue	Caught In The Act	Jazz	
12	☑ Datin' With No Dough	2:28	Royal Crown Revue	Caught In The Act	Jazz	
13	☑ Intro	0:47	Royal Crown Revue	Caught In The Act	Jazz	

HOT TIP: If you don't want to hear a song in a playlist, simply untick the box next to the song name.

Shuffling a playlist

Normally, when you play one song in a playlist, iTunes will continue playing other songs in that same playlist, moving sequentially in whatever sort order you've specified. If the list is alphabetical by album, then you'll hear your songs in that order.

However, often you want to hear random songs. On iTunes, shuffle mode gives you random songs from a playlist.

To turn on shuffling:

1 Select a playlist from the list in the sidebar or click the Music library.

2 Click the Shuffle button in the footer.

3 Play a song. The shuffle mode will pick a song at random to start with, then play other songs randomly after that.

Creating a smart playlist

If you liked smart folders in Finder and smart mailboxes in Mail, then you're really going to like smart playlists in iTunes.

Smart playlists are very similar to other 'smart' objects – instead of creating a static list of songs, you can create criteria that iTunes will use to create a playlist. For example, you might want to build a playlist from a certain year, or that features a certain artist or has a certain rating or play count.

When you build a smart playlist, iTunes adds songs to it automatically and keeps the playlist updated as you grow your music collection.

To create a smart playlist:

1 Choose File > New Smart Playlist from the menu.

2 Choose an item from the first dropdown, such as Artist or Genre.

3 Make appropriate selections from the second and third fields. For example, if you chose Genre, you might choose 'is' from the second dropdown and enter World in the third field.

4 If you have additional criteria, click the + button and add them.

5 Click OK when you've finished.

6 Your new playlist appears in the sidebar. Click the playlist and give it a more appropriate name.

To see the list of songs in a smart playlist, just click on the playlist in the sidebar.

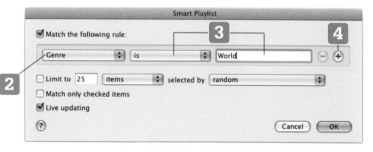

DID YOU KNOW?

iTunes will create various smart playlists for you. For example, one smart playlist is called Purchased and it contains every song you've purchased from the iTunes Store.

Changing the default view of songs in a playlist

Normally, when you click on a playlist or library, you'll see a list of songs with column headers. Each column contains information that helps you identify that song.

However, you can also view your songs in different formats: as a grid of icons or in Cover Flow. The grid of icons shows cover art for that song, while Cover Flow lets you flip through a series of album covers and view column-based details for each song.

To view songs as a grid of icons:

1 Select a playlist or the Music library.

2 Click the grid button (it's on the far right of the toolbar, by the search bar).

To view songs in Cover Flow:

3 Select a playlist or the Music library.

4 Click the Cover Flow button (it's on the far right of the toolbar, by the search bar).

? DID YOU KNOW?

Cover Flow on your Mac is very similar to Cover Flow on your iPod or iPhone. It allows you to quickly browse through your song collection using a visual metaphor.

Adding info to a song

When you buy a song or import it from a CD, you often get lots of information about that song. You'll know the song's name, how long it lasts, what album it was on, its genre, the composer and so on.

Sometimes, though, you end up with incomplete information on a song, or you want to add your own notes.

To add your own information to a song:

1 Choose File > Get Info from the menu, or press ⌘ I on the keyboard.

2 To add comments, click the Info tab and enter your notes under Comments.

3 To add Lyrics, click the Lyrics tab and enter the lyrics for the song.

4 Click OK when you've finished.

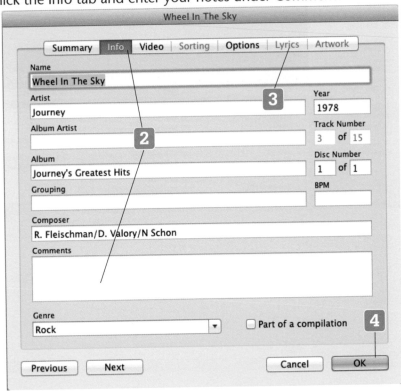

Rating a song

Some songs you'll like more than others. Some songs will remind you of happy times, others will be by a favourite artist or band. It doesn't matter, because iTunes allows you to rate songs from 0 to 5 stars, with 5 being 'best of the best'.

To rate a song, you can do **any** of the following:

1 Click directly on how many stars you want to give it in the Rating column. For example, to give a song four stars, click on the fourth star in the row.

2 Choose File > Rating and then select how many stars to give a song.

3 Control-click a song and choose Rating from the menu, then the number of stars to give it.

? DID YOU KNOW?

There's a smart playlist that ships with iTunes – it's called My Top Rated. It shows your top-rated songs.

Using Genius

So far you've created playlists and smart playlists. Well, get ready for Genius, it's a step beyond smart playlists and will make you wonder how you ever lived without it.

What is Genius? It's simple: all it does is create playlists from songs in your library that go well together. (I'll let you think of all the possibilities for all kinds of great playlists that feature any number of artists and albums.)

Turning on Genius also gives you the Genius Sidebar, which shows items related to the song that's currently playing – a great way to discover new music available on the iTunes Store.

To create a Genius playlist:

1 Select a song in your library.

2 Click the Genius button in the footer (it looks like a bunch of atoms circling each other).

2

3 If the Genius button isn't there, click the Show Genius Sidebar button in the footer (it looks like an arrow pointing to the left) and click Turn On Genius.

4 You may be prompted to log into the iTunes store so that Genius can learn more about you.

5 iTunes will create a Genius playlist from that selected song. To see the songs in the list, click Genius.

6 You can now limit songs in the list by choosing a value from the Limit To dropdown.

7 You can save the playlist by clicking Save Playlist.

8 Your new playlist will be named after the original song you selected.

? **DID YOU KNOW?**
iTunes Genius will only display recommendations for songs, films, TV shows and other products that you don't already own. It's a great way to try out new stuff that goes well with the music and video you already own.

Using iTunes DJ

The iTunes DJ feature allows you to create a 'live mix' of random songs from your entire Music library or selected playlists – and it lets your guests with iPods and iPhones make requests and vote up or down on songs that are currently playing.

To set up iTunes DJ:

1 Under Playlists, click iTunes DJ.

2 Click Continue.

3 To set up a source for the DJ, click the Source dropdown along the bottom of the playlist. You can choose your entire Music library, any smart playlist (including songs you've purchased from the iTunes Store), any Genius playlist or any other playlist.

4 To update your settings, click Settings.

5 To change the number of recently played songs, change the value in the first dropdown.

6 To change the number of upcoming songs, change the value in the second dropdown.

7 Tick the box to allow guests to request songs using Remote for iPhone or iPod Touch.

8 If you like, enter a Welcome message for those remote users.

9 Enable voting by ticking Enable voting.

10 Require a password by ticking the last tickbox and entering a password in the text field.

11 Click OK when you've finished.

> **? DID YOU KNOW?**
> iPhone and iPod Touch owners can download their Remotes free from the App Store.

Syncing an iPod or iPhone

At some point, you'll want to take your music collection with you. Whether you've got an iPod, an iPhone or even a little iPod Shuffle, you can easily sync your iTunes playlists with your mobile devices.

Please note one thing, though: depending on your device, you'll get different options for syncing files. The iPod Shuffle is a much smaller and simpler device than an iPhone – it'll hold only a few hundred songs, whereas an iPhone can hold more than 1000 without a strain.

To sync up a mobile device:

1 Attach the device to your Mac using a USB cable.

2 After a few seconds, the device will appear in the Devices list in the sidebar. For this example, I'm using an iPod Shuffle.

3 Click the device name to see its contents.

4 If you're working with an iPod Shuffle, you can Autofill from just one playlist or smart playlist. For example, I've chosen to keep my iPod Shuffle full of songs I've purchased from the iTunes Store.

5 Click Autofill when you're happy with the selection of songs.

ALERT: Different iPods and devices have different ways to sync up. Please refer to the instructions for your device.

Listening to the radio

You're not limited to listening to your own music or buying songs from the iTunes Store. You can also use iTunes to listen to Internet radio stations. It's a great way to listen to talk radio, current hits, golden oldies or whatever you want to listen to.

To listen to a radio station:

1 Under Library, click Radio.

2 iTunes displays a number of categories, like Alternative, Comedy, Country, Latino, Rock and Sports.

3 Click one of the categories to display the available streams (or radio station).

4 Double-click a radio station to hear its 'broadcast' on the Internet.

Burn a playlist to CD

You've got your playlists, smart playlists, Genius collections and more, and now you want to burn a CD of your favourite tracks. Thankfully, iTunes lets you do just that with its Burn Disc feature.

To burn a CD:

1 Insert a blank CD into your Mac's optical drive.

2 Choose a playlist, smart playlist or Genius playlist.

3 Click Burn Disc.

4 Choose the type of CD: Audio (which can be played in a car or stereo CD player), MP3 CD or Data CD or DVD.

5 Click Burn when you're ready.

! ALERT: iTunes will warn you if you're trying to burn too many songs onto a CD.

Share your music with others

If you're working on the same wireless network with another Mac (whether at home, work or in a coffee shop, for example), you might want to make your Music library available for others to listen to. It's an easy way to let others know exactly what your music taste is.

When you share a playlist, it shows up under Shared in the other person's iTunes sidebar.

To share your music:

1 Choose iTunes > Preferences from the menu.

2 Click the Sharing tab.

3 Select 'Share my library on my local network'.

4 If you want to limit who can see your music with a password, select Require password and enter a password.

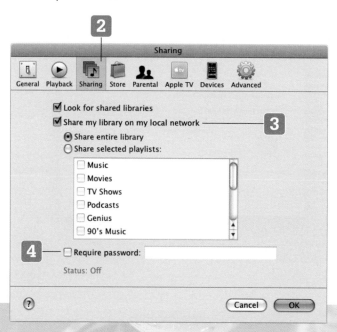

? DID YOU KNOW?

If your computer is off or iTunes isn't running, then others can't share your music.

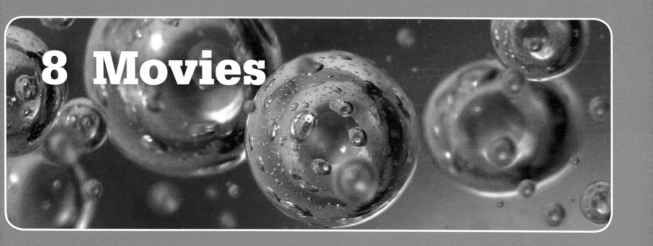

8 Movies

Introduction

Your Mac doesn't just help you keep in touch with friends, organise photos and music, and keep track of all your appointments, it's also got a built-in movie studio called iMovie.

iMovie is a fast and easy way to turn your home video into your own movies. It works with the latest digital HD movie cameras, video from camera phones and any other type of device that captures video, like your Mac's iSight camera.

With iMovie, you can edit video, add titles and background music, create transitions and share your projects by publishing them to DVD or YouTube.

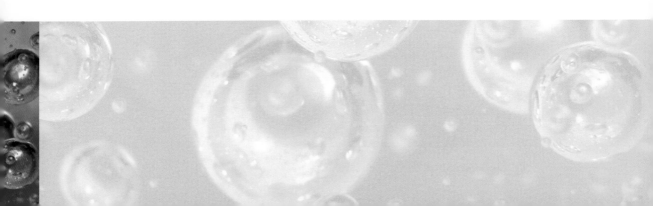

Starting iMovie

iMovie is an easy-to-use movie-editing tool that allows you to import and edit footage from a digital video camera, add soundtracks, add titles and much, much more. But before you can enjoy any of its slick features, you've got to fire up iMovie!

To start iMovie:

- Click the iMovie icon on the Dock (if it's on the Dock).
- Alternatively, open the Applications folder and double-click iMovie.

When you first start iMovie, click the Create a New Project button and give your new project a name (like 'My Movie') to get started.

When iMovie opens, you'll see a main viewing screen on the right. Below that is where your video clips will show up when you import them from a camera. To the left of the viewing screen is the timeline, which is how your movie is organised. Sandwiched in between are a few editing tools.

? DID YOU KNOW?

You can also create a Magic Movie. I won't cover it here, because it's pretty intuitive. When you're feeling confident enough, why not click it to see what happens?

Importing video from your video camera

Now that you've got iMovie started up, it's time to do some work with your video. You've probably already shot some digital video with a digital video camera. In fact, if you're anything like me, you can't stop shooting video – my wife and I have just purchased a Flip HD and used it to shoot countless scenes of our last road trip through the American southwest.

Well, you probably also have lots of footage. Here's how to get it off your camera and into iMovie:

1 Follow all the instructions for connecting your particular brand of digicam, digital movie camera or HD camera. You might need a particular kind of cable (USB or FireWire, for example).

2 When you connect a video camera, you should see the Import window.

3 Click a clip and press play to review a clip.

4 You can click Import All to import all the video.

5 If you want to import just a few clips, switch to manual, select your clips and then click Import.

6 When you import, don't forget to give your clips an Event name. For example, they could be videos of a certain trip, an occasion like a birthday party, or whatever.

7 Once you've done that, click Import.

8 When you've finished importing video from your camera, turn off the camera and eject it from the computer.

? **DID YOU KNOW?**

You may already have video loaded onto your Mac. To import those segments into iMovie, choose File > Import from the menu.

Reviewing imported clips

Each clip or scene that's imported from a camera or your Mac's hard drive is added to the bottom pane of the iMovie interface. You can review each clip very easily to see what you might want to include in your overall movie project.

To review an imported clip:

1 Hover your mouse over a clip, moving right to left to review a clip.

2 Click the Full Screen button to view the clip in full-screen mode.

? **DID YOU KNOW?**

You can review more than one clip at a time by selecting multiple ones by Shift or Command clicking, then pressing the space bar.

Adding clips to the timeline

Once you've reviewed your clips, it's time to start putting together a rough movie. Luckily for you, iMovie provides a really simple tool for building a movie project: it's called a timeline and it represents a chronological stream that you can add your clips to.

To add clips to the timeline:

1 Click anywhere in the clips you've imported.

2 iMovie will select a four-second strip within the clip.

3 You can drag that four-second clip up into your project.

4 If you want more or less than four seconds, simply drag the ends of the selection.

5 Drag your selection to the timeline below the editing tools.

? DID YOU KNOW?

You can tell which sections you've already used because they'll be marked with an orange bar.

Deleting clips

Every once in a while, you'll review a clip and wonder, 'Well, what was the point of shooting that video?' You know what I'm talking about here – an entire 30 seconds of video (with lens cap still firmly in place), or shots of you holding a camera as you run down the stairs (it's enough to make anyone sick to their stomach) and so on.

For these clips, there's no point trying to find anything to salvage. To delete the entire clip:

1 Select the clip.

2 Choose Edit > Cut from the menu or press the Delete key.

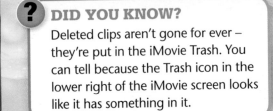

DID YOU KNOW?

Deleted clips aren't gone for ever – they're put in the iMovie Trash. You can tell because the Trash icon in the lower right of the iMovie screen looks like it has something in it.

Cropping clips

Chances are, you'll have some clips with something salvageable in them. However, you might have long stretches where the subject of interest is far away in the shot, or something weird is happening in a foreground corner of the shot that is too distracting.

Don't fret, because here's where cropping can really help.

To crop a clip:

1 Select a clip.

2 Click the Action button (it looks like a gear in the lower left of the clip) and choose Cropping & Rotation from the dropdown menu.

3 Click Crop.

4 Use the drag handles to resize the frame.

5 Click Done.

To undo your changes:

- Choose Edit > Undo.
- Alternatively, press ⌘ Z on the keyboard.

ALERT: There's a limit to how much you can crop a clip. If you shoot in high definition, you'll have a lot less chance of ending up with grainy footage, but even so, the rule is simple: the more you crop, the more chance you have of getting grainy footage.

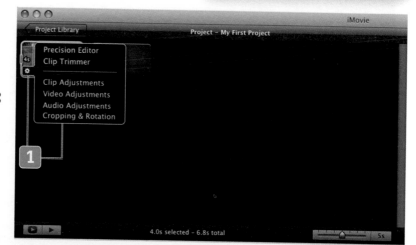

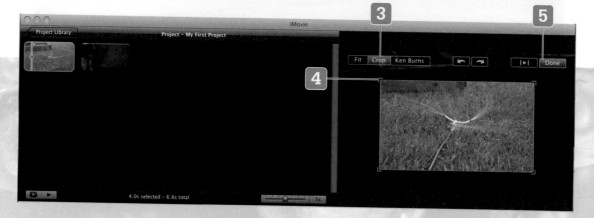

Reordering clips

Whether your clips are in the clip viewer to the right of the main screen or already placed in the timeline, you can put them in any order you prefer.

Being able to move clips around gives you a great deal of artistic flexibility. You can mix clips up, altering the way events actually occurred. You can cut back and forth between two sets of events, giving you the freedom to shape a storyline. You get the idea.

To reorder a clip:

1 Hold your mouse down on a clip.

2 Use your mouse to drag into a new position on the timeline or the clip viewer.

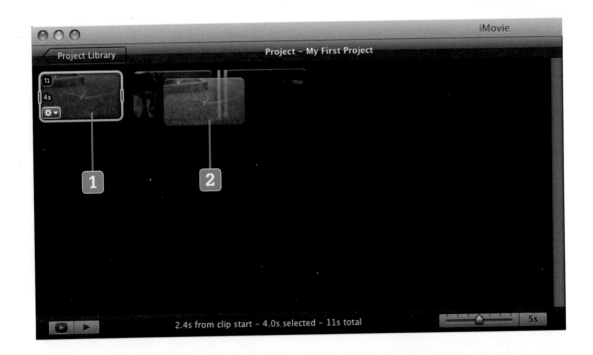

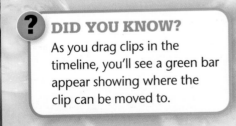

DID YOU KNOW?

As you drag clips in the timeline, you'll see a green bar appear showing where the clip can be moved to.

Trimming clips

Once you've got clips on the timeline, you'll notice that certain things don't seem to flow right. You'll want to make lots of small (and large) adjustments now that everything is together in one flow. One adjustment you can make is called trimming.

To trim a clip:

1 Make a selection of frames in one or more clips.

2 Choose Edit > Trim to Selection from the menu.

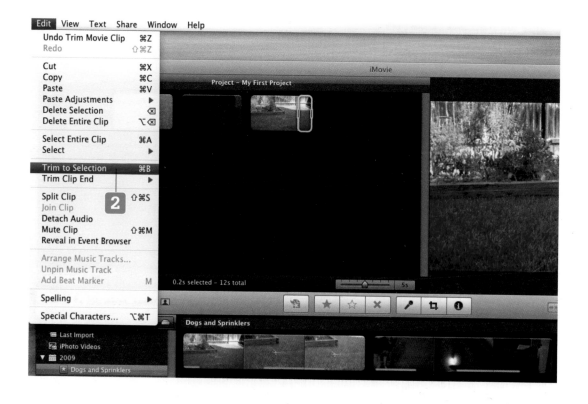

Splitting clips

Yet another way to edit a clip is to split it in two. Why would you want to do that? Well, you might want to take a long clip and insert a title in between the action, or add photos or other clips in between the action of the longer clip.

To split a clip:

1 Use your mouse to drag a selection from one or more clips.

2 Choose Edit > Split Clip from the menu.

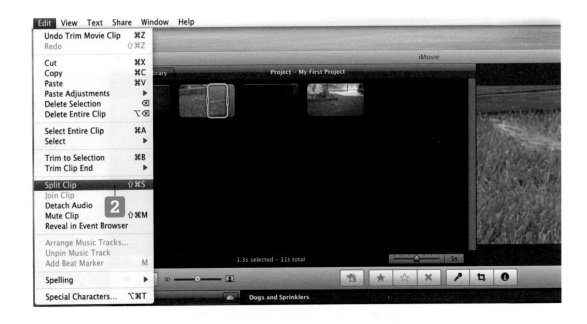

DID YOU KNOW?

iMovie keeps track of all your original footage, even the ones you've cropped, so it's possible to retrieve your original, uncut, unmodified footage at any time.

Saving your movie project

You may be used to saving your work constantly to guard against bad things happening, but iMovie saves your work automatically. Every time you make a change, iMovie takes notice and saves it so there is no requirement for you to do this. Therefore, the screenshot below shows no Save option in the File menu.

 HOT TIP: You can also roll back the clock by reverting to a last saved version of a project. Why would you do this? Well, let's say you make a lot of changes that turn out to be a bad decision. Just choose File > Revert to Saved from the menu and you're back to where you were before you made all those wrong changes.

Adding titles to your movie

iMovie lets you add titles, credits and other text to your project, giving it the kind of additional polish that you see in professional documentaries and films.

To add a title:

1 Click the Titles button.

2 Drag the title style you want to your project timeline.

3 Type your title text in the text field below the list of titles.

4 The title clip is updated in your project.

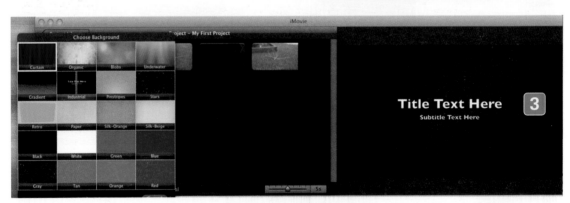

Creating transitions

Now that you've added clips, moved them around, trimmed them, split them and added titles, you may notice that some of your changes from scene to scene seem pretty abrupt, while others are long and boring and lack visual interest.

Thankfully, iMovie gives you a great deal of control over transitions. With transitions, you can blend the ends of clips together in interesting ways. For example, you can fade from one scene to the next, or use dissolves or pushes.

To add a transition between scenes:

1 Click the Transitions button in the toolbar, or choose Window > Transitions from the menu.

2 You can preview the transitions by hovering over them in the list with your mouse.

3 Drag the transition you want between any two video clips.

4 To adjust the timing on a transition, double-click a transition icon in your project and edit the Duration period.

5 Remember that you can make changes to all transitions at once. If you don't want your changes applied globally, untick the box next to Applies to all transitions.

6 If you change your mind about the kind of transition you have in place, simply choose a new one from the Transition dropdown.

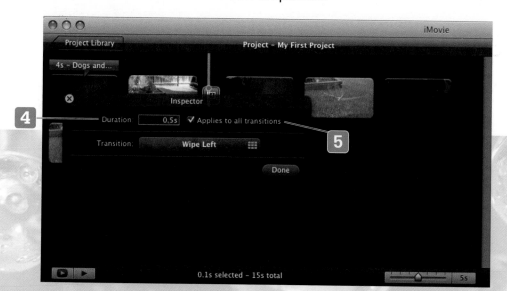

Adding music and audio

Imagine going to a movie and having to sit through one that didn't have a powerful soundtrack. Or imagine watching a documentary that didn't have some kind of voiceover explaining what was happening in certain scenes.

As you can tell, a good music soundtrack or audio track can add a lot to a movie, setting the right tone and adding depth. Of course, when you import a video clip, you also get whatever sound the video camera recorded, which you can also adjust.

To add audio to your movie project:

1 Click the Audio button in the toolbar.

2 Click one of your audio sources – usually Garage Band or iTunes.

3 Drag a song into your project, but make sure it lands in one of the background areas.

Adding photos to your movie

Of course, you don't have to have movie clips to make a movie – sometimes you can get some pretty neat effects just using the images you've got stored in iPhoto. iMovie lets you add photos; it even lets you pan and zoom in or out with the celebrated Ken Burns effect.

To add photos:

1 Click the Photos button in the toolbar.

2 Drag whatever photos you want to use into your project, positioning them in the proper sequence.

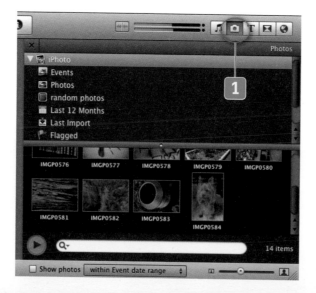

Adding effects to photos

Every image has its own Photo Settings window that you can use to add various effects to a photo.

To add effects to a photo:

1 Click a photo, then click the Action button in the lower left (it looks like a gear).

2 Choose Cropping, Ken Burns & Rotation from the dropdown menu.

3 Drag and resize the Start box to where you want your image to be when the effect starts.

4 Drag and resize the End box to where you want your image to be when the effect ends.

5 Click Done.

Depending on how you set up the effects, the Ken Burns effect will pan and zoom from the start state to the end state.

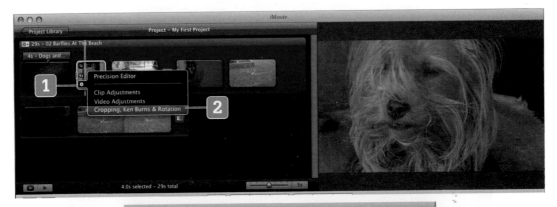

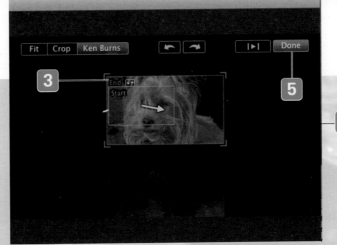

Adding a theme template to your movie

Instead of manually selecting title styles and visual effects (which you may not have the time or patience for), you might want to select a theme template. Themes in iMovie add Hollywood-style polish to your movie, giving it a more unified design with animated graphics, great backgrounds and title styles that will impress everyone who sees your final project.

To use a theme:

1. Choose File > Project Properties from the menu.

2. You can preview any theme by moving your mouse over a theme's preview thumbnail.

3. Choose a theme by clicking it and clicking OK.

4. Click the theme title above the first clip and edit the title on the theme. Please note that you may need to delete a title clip if you've previously added it.

Slowing down, speeding up and reversing the video

What's a movie without special visual effects? We all know from watching movies that directors use slow motion, fast motion and reverse video for different dramatic and humorous effects. You can do the same thing with iMovie.

To apply a special effect to a clip:

1 Double-click any clip.

2 To slow it down, move the speed slider to the left.

3 To speed it up, move the speed slider to the right.

4 To reverse the clip, tick the Reverse box.

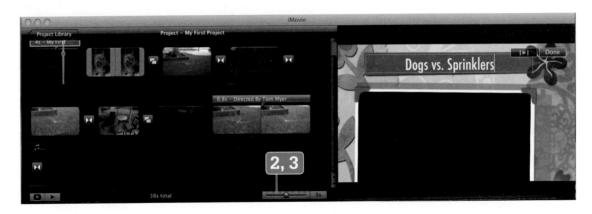

> **? DID YOU KNOW?**
> If you don't see the speed slider,
> click Convert the Entire Clip.

Stabilising shaky video

Sometimes it's hard to keep the camera steady and you can end up with shaky video. Maybe you sneezed when you were shooting the clip, or the car you were travelling in was going down a bumpy road. Doesn't matter, because iMovie can help remove some of that shakiness with its stabilisation features.

To stabilise any shaky video:

1 Select all the video in the clip viewer (not the project!) and choose File > Analyze for Stabilization from the menu. You can do this for an entire movie or for individual clips.

2 iMovie will add a wavy red line to any video that is too shaky to use. You can hide all of that video by clicking the Hide Shaky Video button (it looks like a wavy red line).

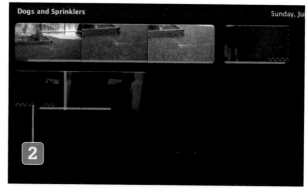

3 All other video will have its video smoothed out automatically.

Sharing your movie with others

Now that you've got your movie all finished, it doesn't do you any good to have it sitting on your computer, now does it? You need to share your efforts with friends, family and others. iMovie lets you share your movie in many different ways.

For example, you can:

- Send it to others via email.
- Publish it to the Web using iWeb.
- Transfer it to an iPod or iPhone.
- Burn it to a DVD.
- Save it as a QuickTime movie with a variety of settings.
- Upload it to YouTube.

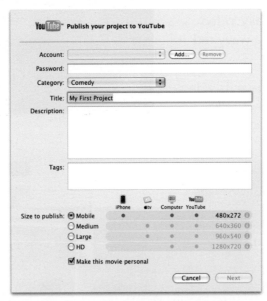

To share your movie:

- Choose Share on the iMovie menu, then select the appropriate method.

DID YOU KNOW?

Every minute, users around the world add 20 hours of video to Youtube.com!

9 Building websites

Introduction

If you thought that building websites was something only the cool digital kids could do, well, you're mistaken! Your Mac comes with an elegant, easy-to-use website creation tool called iWeb. You can use other tools to create websites (like Dreamweaver or BBEdit) but iWeb is certainly the easiest for the beginner.

When you work with iWeb, you can see what each webpage will look like when it's published. You can apply ready-made themes to give your site a professional look in minutes, add Google Maps, custom HTML, images, create a blog and more, then publish it all with the touch of a button.

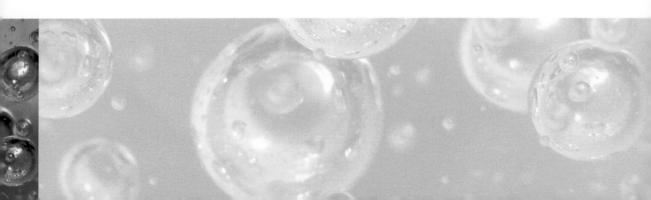

Starting up iWeb

Creating websites with iWeb is very simple: you can start with a theme and then customise your website with pages full of content, photos, music and video. You can even add Google Maps, ads and your own custom HTML if you like.

To get started:

- Click the iWeb icon in the Dock (if it's in the Dock).
- Alternatively, navigate to the Applications folder and double-click iWeb.

When you first open iWeb, you'll see a screen divided into these main sections:

- The sidebar contains all the websites you've created, and under each website, a list of pages for each site.
- The main canvas displays one page at a time in WYSIWYG (What You See Is What You Get) layout, with placeholder text and images. The site will include navigation links that match the title and order of pages in your site – iWeb will keep this navigation current as you make changes to your site.
- Below the canvas is a toolbar that gives you access to key functionality: themes, shapes, fonts and more.
- Below that is the iWeb footer, which lets you add pages or publish your site at the touch of a button.
- To the far right is your media browser, which includes audio, photos, movies and widgets.

Creating a site

Okay, it's time to create a website. If you have any friends who are web designers (or have worked with anyone who is a web designer) then you probably think that creating a website is a big deal – that it involves lots of planning, excruciating detail and tons of coding.

Well, that may be true of a huge corporate website, but for the site you're going to build with iWeb, it's not really a big deal. In fact, if you're putting together a personal website, blog, travel journal, photo journal or small business site, iWeb is ideal, mostly because it's fast and easy.

To create a site:

1. Start iWeb.

2. If you've created a site before, choose File > New Site from the menu.

3. If not, then just choose a Theme for your new site from the window.

4. Your new site will appear in the sidebar – it's called Site.

5. Your new site will have a single page called Welcome. This is your site's home page.

Using the themed templates

When you created your site, iWeb prompted you to select a theme for your site. A theme is a unified set of templates that gives your website a slick, professional look. It includes everything from the layout and typography to link colours and background images.

Just because you set up a site with a certain theme doesn't mean that you're stuck with that theme for ever. In fact, you can change a site's theme by doing the following:

1 Click on any page in your site. If you've just started a new site, the only page in the site will be the Welcome page.

2 Click the Theme button in the toolbar and select a new theme from the list.

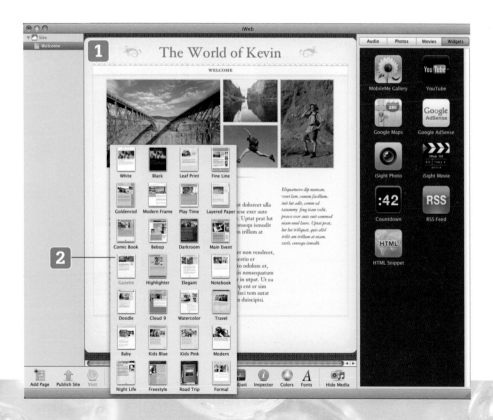

? DID YOU KNOW?

You can have different themes for each page on your site, although this isn't really a good idea as it can confuse your website visitors and cause the design of your site to spiral out of control. In design, less is more – choose a theme and stick with it on all your pages.

Adding pages to your site

Now that you have a new site under way, it's time to start adding pages. I like to take this step first because it helps me plan out my website.

For example, most websites have an 'about us' page, a 'contact us' page and other pages that describe different aspects of the company or their life. iWeb comes with various types of pages you can add, like a Photos page, a Movie page, a Podcast page and a general-purpose blank page. It all depends, of course, on which theme you've set for your site.

To add a page to your site:

1 Click the Add Page button in the footer.

2 Select a page from the list provided by iWeb.

3 Click Choose.

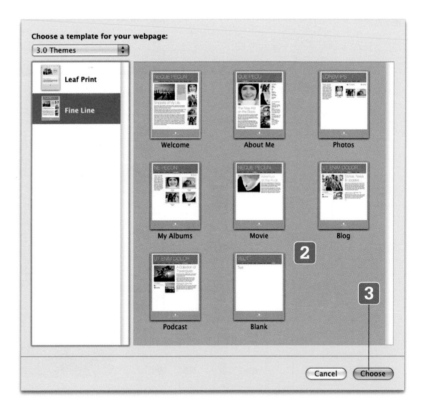

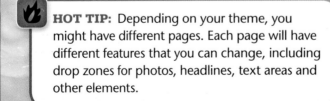

HOT TIP: Depending on your theme, you might have different pages. Each page will have different features that you can change, including drop zones for photos, headlines, text areas and other elements.

Adding text to your site

On a website, content is king, and text is a very important part of that equation. Although you'll probably have photos and video on your site, most of what will hold the site together will be text. You can add text to your website in two ways using iWeb.

- The first involves simply double-clicking on an existing block of text provided by a template and editing the text that is already there.
- The second involves clicking Text Box in the toolbar and then drawing a rectangle with your mouse to add a text field to the site that you can fill in with your own copy.

 ALERT: Some templates may not allow you to add new text boxes.

 DID YOU KNOW?
You can normally resize any block of text by clicking it once and then dragging one of its selection handles.

Adding images to your site

Another big part of your site will be photos. They might be from your personal collection, or they might be some stock or professional photography that you've purchased for the purpose of making your site look better.

Either way, you can easily work with photos and other images in iWeb.

To add images:

1 First, click Show Media in the toolbar if you don't see it to the right. This opens the Media Browser.

2 Click Photos at the top of the Media Browser.

3 Select a roll, album or library.

4 Select an image and drag it to a placeholder image in your themed template. When you see the plus sign appear, release the image.

? DID YOU KNOW?

These placeholder images are considered 'drop zones' that will accept other images in their place.

? DID YOU KNOW?

You can also drag images from your Desktop or any Finder window.

Adding masks to images

Sometimes your photos and other images are too big for their designated spot in a layout. Did you notice, however, that iWeb did a pretty good job of making that image work? You might be dropping a square image into a slot that is very wide but not too tall, but it worked out all right.

Why? Because iWeb uses masks for most photos in the layout. Think of a mask as a way to control what part of the image you can see. For example, you might find yourself dragging your photos into a theme and seeing only the most uninteresting part of the photo. This isn't your fault – it was a great picture but you ran into a weird or unintended shape.

To adjust the mask on a picture:

1 Click a picture.

2 Click Edit Mask.

3 Adjust the zoom on the picture using the Zoom slider.

4 Click Edit Mask.

You can now drag the image right to left and bottom to top to adjust what you see through the mask provided by iWeb. It's a little like moving a picture inside a frame while the mounting is still in place.

Adding photo galleries to your site

Not only does iWeb allow you to simply drag and drop individual images and photos to your site, you can also set up photo gallery pages that automate the process of setting up slide shows and clickable galleries with thumbnails.

To add a photo gallery to your site:

1 Click the Add Page button in the footer.

2 Select the Photos page in the list of pages and click Choose.

3 Drag an entire iPhoto album or roll onto the new page.

4 Make any adjustments you need in the Photo Grid dialogue box.

You now have a page built with thumbnails that link to a bigger picture and a link to a smooth-running slide show of your album.

? DID YOU KNOW?

iWeb will automatically create a grid of photos for you, with a maximum count of 99 photos per page. If you have more than your allotted maximum per page, iWeb automatically paginates the photos for you.

Adding music and audio files to your site

Although you may (rightfully, mind you) think that sites with music playing on them are annoying, consider this: not all audio files are music and not all music files are annoying.

Now that we have that little Zen koan out of the way, you're probably wondering, 'What in the devil is he talking about?' Well, it's simple: you might want to share a podcast or audio recording you've made, or a bunch of sound effects, or yes, some music that you've just created with your band.

To add music to your site:

1 First, click Show Media in the toolbar. This opens the Media Browser.

2 Click Audio at the top of the Media Browser.

3 Select a playlist from iTunes or a set of sound files from Garage Band.

4 Select an audio file and drag it to an empty part of a page.

5 iWeb will add an audio player to the page and prompt you to add an image that goes with that song.

Adding video to your site

Nowadays, no site is complete without some kind of video on it and iWeb doesn't disappoint here either. You can easily create Movie pages with just about any theme, adding a more captivating interactive dimension to your site with your iMovie creations.

To add video to your site:

1 Click the Add Page button in the toolbar.

2 Select the Movie page and click Choose.

3 Click the Media button in the toolbar.

4 Click Movies.

5 Choose a movie project from iMovie or a video clip from Photo Booth. You can also click Widgets and drag a YouTube widget onto the page, then enter the URL for the YouTube video you'd like to add.

6 Drag your movie to the placeholder on the page.

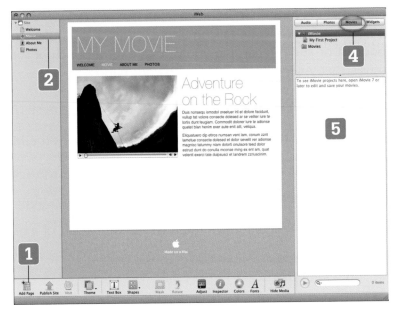

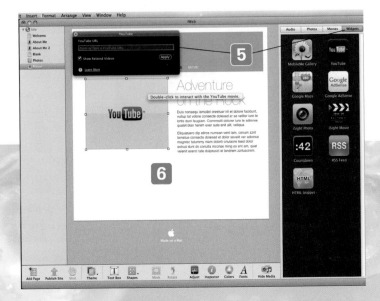

Adding maps to your site

How many times have you visited a website for a company or event and wondered out loud, 'Well, why can't they just put a map on their "about us" page so we can find where they are?' I mean, seriously, a good set of directions is a nice thing, but a map just completes it.

iWeb solves this problem by offering you a set of Web Widgets, one of which is the ability to integrate Google Maps directly into your website.

To add a map:

1 Make sure you're connected to the Internet.

2 Click the Widgets button in the Media Browser and drag the Google Maps onto a page or choose Insert > Widget > Google Map from the menu.

3 In the Google Map that appears, type the address and click Apply.

4 In the Google Map, select the tickboxes to set whether your site visitors can see the zoom controls and the address bubble. It's a good idea to enable both.

5 Drag the map to where you want it on the page.

6 Use the drag handles to resize the map once it's in the right place.

7 You can zoom in and out and pan around to give your visitors a better idea of what you're showing.

? DID YOU KNOW?
You can easily delete a map by clicking on it and pressing the Delete key.

Adding ads to your site

You can easily turn your website into a little income generator by adding another Web Widget to your site: Google Adsense. The Google Adsense program allows you to insert ads on your webpages that are relevant to the surrounding content on the page.

For example, if you've got a page that describes your recent holiday to Spain, then the ads should all be about travel packages, Spain and so on. You earn revenue (usually in small increments) from Google every time a visitor to your site clicks on one of the ads.

To add a Google Adsense ad to your site:

1 Click Widgets in the Media Browser and then drag Google Adsense onto a page, or choose Insert > Widget > Google Adsense Ad from the menu.

2 When the dialogue box pops up, you can do one of the following:

- If you already have a Google Adsense account, click I Already Have An Account and then sign into your Google Adsense account.

- If you don't have an account, type the email address you want to use and click Submit.

3 Place the ad (it will be a placeholder ad) where you want it on the page.

? DID YOU KNOW?

Ads will begin appearing on your site within 48 hours. In the meantime, Google will place public-service ads on your site. Also, please note that actual ads are visible only on a published website, not in iWeb!

Adding shapes

iWeb allows you to add different kinds of shapes to your sites, such as rectangles, triangles, arrows, circles, stars, conversation bubbles and more. What's more, you can apply different colours to those shapes and even add text to them.

You can use these shapes to create diagrams, to illustrate your web content, or to call out photos (for example, using an arrow to point to one specific person in a group shot).

To add a shape:

- Click the Shapes button on the toolbar and then pick a shape.
- Alternatively, choose Insert > Shape and then choose a shape from the list.

A shape will appear on your page. You can place the shape by dragging it with your mouse. Use the drag handles to resize the shape. Click inside the shape once and start typing to add text.

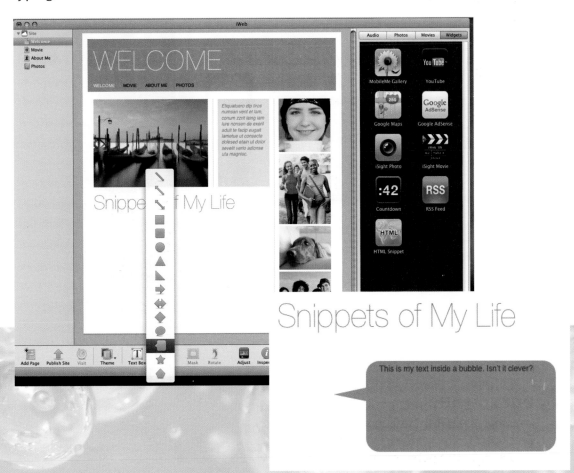

Adding custom HTML

Sometimes you have to add material to your website that goes beyond the point-and-click convenience of everything we've covered so far in this chapter. You might need to add a snippet of Javascript to make something work. Or you've got a particularly weird layout that requires some custom HTML markup.

Luckily, iWeb allows you to add any kind of HTML or code snippet that you need. Here's how to do it:

1 Click the Widgets button in the Media Broswer and drag HTML Snippet onto a page or choose Insert > Widget > HTML Snippet.

2 Copy and paste or type your custom HTML into the box provided.

3 Click Apply.

? DID YOU KNOW?

Javascript and HTML are languages used by web developers to create interactivity on a website.

Adding links to a page

The Web is all about links, right? It was the appearance of those little blue underlined words back in the early 1990s that made the Web take off like it did. Suddenly, you didn't need to know any arcane commands to go from one place to another – all you had to do was click with your mouse.

Simple, brilliant and easy.

iWeb allows you to add links just as easily – you don't need to know any code at all!

To add a link:

1 Select some text or an image that will become a link.

2 Choose Insert > Hyperlink from the menu and then choose the type of link you want to add:

- A webpage link goes to either one of your own pages or a page on another site.
- An email link opens an email message to a specific email address.
- A file link opens a specific file that's on your own website.

3 You'll see a dialogue box that will guide you to make the right selection. For example, if you've selected email link, you'll be prompted to enter an email address and subject line. If you've selected a file link, you'll be prompted to choose a file on your Mac. If you've selected a webpage link, you'll be prompted to choose an internal page or an external webpage link.

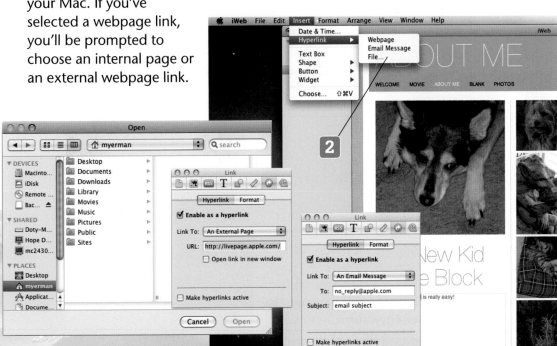

Duplicating a page

It's very easy to add pages to your site in iWeb, but sometimes you work really hard on a page and get it just so, then need another page that's very similar to it. There's no need to create the new page from scratch when you can simply duplicate the existing page and then make your minor changes to the new page.

To duplicate a page, do one of the following:

- On the sidebar, control-click the page you want to duplicate and choose Duplicate from the pop-up menu.
- Choose a page on the sidebar and choose Edit > Duplicate from the menu.
- Choose a page on the sidebar and press ⌘ D on the keyboard.

 HOT TIP: Your new page will have a name similar to the original page. To rename a page, simply click the name once, wait a moment, then click again. When the background on the name changes, enter a new name.

Reorganising the navigation

Now that you've got a few pages up on the site, you notice that your navigation seems a bit out of order. You feel that some pages shouldn't be on the navigation at all, while others should be last in the list instead of in the middle (or vice versa).

In iWeb, you don't make changes to navigation directly in the editing window. Instead, you rearrange the pages in the sidebar. Whatever changes you make there, iWeb will make happen on the navigation component of your theme automatically.

To reorganise pages in the navigation:

● On the sidebar, drag a page to a new spot in the order.

You'll notice the navigation update immediately once you make your changes.

As you drag a page, you will see a locator bar appear to indicate where your page is going to be moved to. You can see this locator bar in the image below.

? DID YOU KNOW?

You can easily take a page off the navigation menu. This is a great thing if you have 'secret' pages that you don't want everyone to know about. To remove a page from navigation, select it in the sidebar, then click the Inspector in the toolbar. Once the Inspector is open, click the Page Inspector button (it looks like a page) and then untick Include in navigation menu.

Deleting pages from your site

Working on a website isn't just about adding words, photos, music and movies – sometimes you also have to clear out old pages that no longer contain anything you want to keep.

To delete a page, do one of the following:

- On the sidebar, control-click the page you want to delete and choose Delete Page from the pop-up menu.
- Choose a page on the sidebar and choose Edit > Delete Page from the menu.

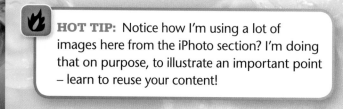

HOT TIP: Notice how I'm using a lot of images here from the iPhoto section? I'm doing that on purpose, to illustrate an important point – learn to reuse your content!

Renaming your site

At this point your website still has a goofy name like 'Site' or whatever. Since you probably want the site's name to be a bit more descriptive than that, let's go ahead and change it.

To rename your site, do one of the following:

- On the sidebar, control-click the site name and click Rename from the pop-up menu.
- Single-click the site name, wait a moment, then click again.

When the background on the site name changes colour, enter a new name.

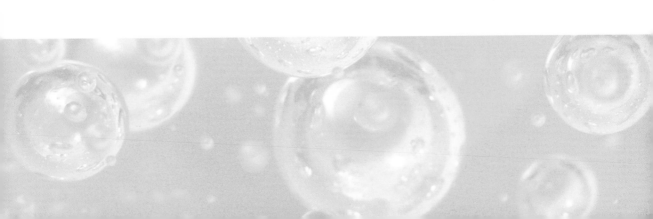

Publishing your website

At some point you'll be ready to share your genius with the world. I mean, what's the use of having a website if the only person who gets to see it is you and your cat?

iWeb offers various publishing options that make it easy for you to publish your site on the World Wide Web.

To publish your site:

1 Click your site name in the sidebar.

2 Choose your publishing option in the Publish to dropdown.

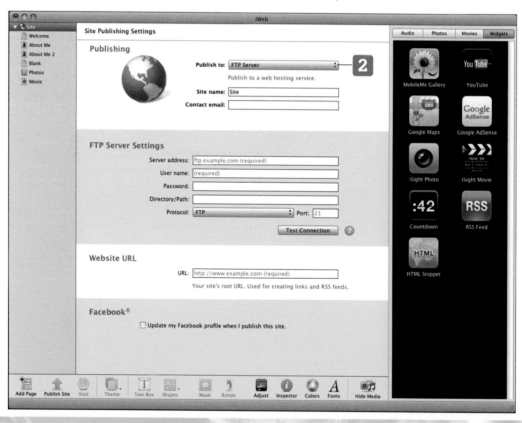

3 For example, if you have a MobileMe account, provide your login credentials.

4 If you've hosted your site with a hosting company, they'll need to provide you with certain details to make the FTP transfer work. You'll need to know:

- The server's hostname or IP address.
- Your user name and password.
- Other settings as needed (for example, whether you'll need to use secure FTP or passive FTP).

Your hosting company's IT help desk should be able to walk you through any questions you might have.

WHAT DOES THIS MEAN?

FTP: File Transfer Protocol. It's how you transfer files from your computer to a web server that runs your website. In order to use FTP you'll need a user name and password from your hosting company.

MobileMe: Service offered by Apple for storing files and documents, including music and images. You can run an entire website if you like! To sign up for an account, visit the Apple website.

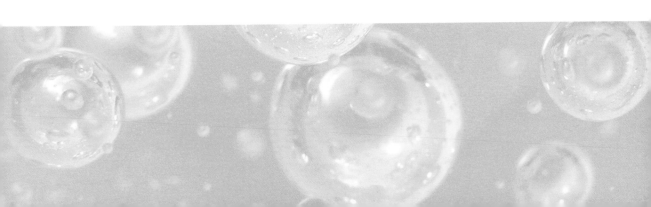

10 Customising your Mac

Introduction

Now that you own a Mac and you've learned how to use the most popular applications and features on it, don't forget that you have the ultimate flexibility to configure and customise your computer the way you want it to be.

In this chapter, you're going to learn how to do exactly that, using the built-in System Preferences.

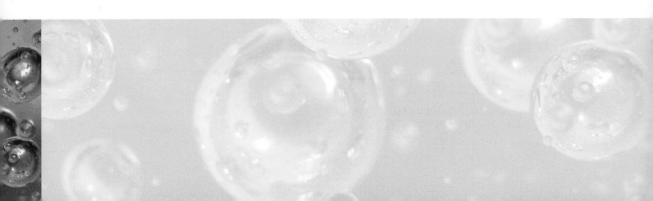

Opening System Preferences

On a Mac, you control your environment through a tool called System Preferences. System Preferences contains all kinds of widgets and buttons that allow you to change your Desktop background, adjust your screen resolution, manage users, manage security and sharing features, and much, much more.

All of it is conveniently available to you by clicking on the Apple icon in the upper left of your screen and choosing System Preferences from the menu.

When you first open System Preferences, you'll see:

1 A top toolbar that allows you to navigate back and forth and a search bar for finding tools and utilities faster.

2 A series of rows, each containing a set of related tools.

- The top row features personal preferences like the Dock and screen saver.
- The second row features hardware preferences like Displays and Mice.
- The third row features Internet and networking preferences.
- The fourth row features system preferences such as user accounts, date and time, and Time Machine.

3 You may have other rows that contain buttons that control the preferences of various downloaded programs.

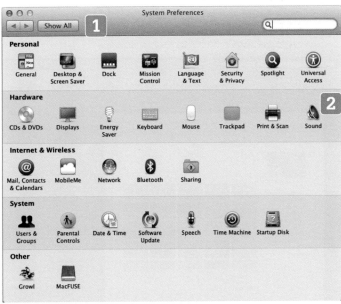

? DID YOU KNOW?

You can add System Preferences to your Dock after you launch it. Just control-click the System Preferences icon in the Dock and choose Keep in Dock from the pop-up menu.

Creating a screen saver

When you're not busy working on your Mac, you probably don't want to just leave the screen sitting there, showing your Desktop or whatever file you're working on. It would be a lot better to show all the lovely pictures you've organised in iPhoto.

To create a screen saver:

1 Select System Preferences from the Apple menu.

2 Click Desktop & Screen Saver.

3 Click Screen Saver at the top of the screen.

4 If you've got a lot of music in your collection, try the iTunes Artwork inside the Apple folder. You'll get to see cover art of your favourite music.

5 If you've got a lot of photos in iPhoto or in folders, use one of the options under Pictures to select images. You can even select images from an RSS feed or MobileMe.

6 Choose a style:

- One image at a time in a slide show format.
- Images jumbled artfully on the screen as a collage.
- A dynamic mosaic.

7 Set the time to wait before the screen saver starts.

8 You can test your screen saver by clicking Test.

9 Close System Preferences by clicking the red button in the upper left corner of the window.

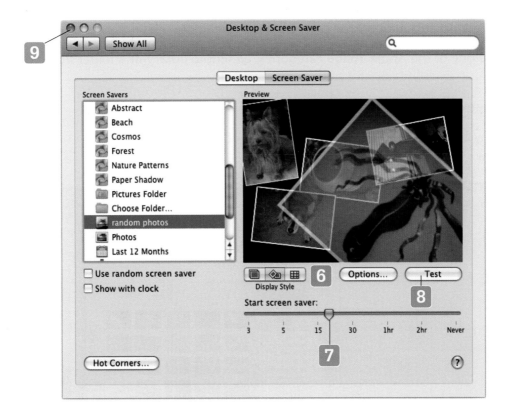

ALERT: If you choose Mosaic as the screen saver type, please be aware that you might experience a slight delay as your Mac composes the initial image.

Changing your Desktop background

As lovely as your default Mac Desktop background is, you probably don't want to keep it around for ever, right? Well, it's pretty easy to change it.

To change your Desktop background:

1 Select System Preferences from the Apple menu.

2 Click Desktop & Screen Saver.

3 Click Desktop at the top of the screen.

4 Choose one of the Apple image categories, an iPhoto library or a folder from your Mac.

5 Click one of the images from that group.

6 Close System Preferences by clicking the red button in the upper left corner of the window.

? DID YOU KNOW?

You can also get to this screen by control-clicking the Desktop and choosing Change Desktop Background from the pop-up menu.

Customising security options

Depending on your situation, you're going to have different security needs. Luckily for you, your Mac can easily be configured to be as wide open (or as secure!) as you wish it to be.

To customise your security options:

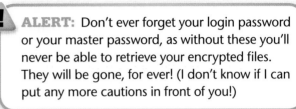

> **ALERT:** Don't ever forget your login password or your master password, as without these you'll never be able to retrieve your encrypted files. They will be gone, for ever! (I don't know if I can put any more cautions in front of you!)

1 Select System Preferences from the Apple menu.

2 Click Security.

3 Click General.

4 If you want to secure your computer while it is sleeping or playing a screen saver, tick the box next to Require password to wake this computer from sleep or screen saver.

5 Click FileVault.

6 If you want to secure your home folder with powerful encryption, turn on FileVault. FileVault will encrypt your files using your login password. Be very careful about using this feature!

7 Click Firewall.

8 You can control who has remote access to your Mac by changing these settings. It's a good idea to at the very least choose the radio button next to Allow only essential services.

9 Close System Preferences by clicking the red button in the upper left corner of the window.

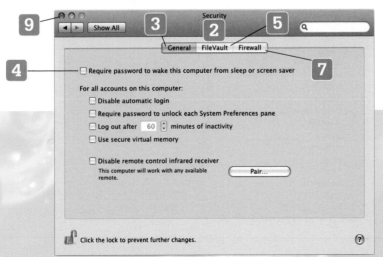

Changing your language settings

When you first took that lovely, shiny new Mac out of the box and set it up, you made a decision about what language to use. Well, depending on what part of the world you're in, you may be seeing the right language, but other things might be slightly off – like where the commas show up in currency readings and that sort of thing.

To change your language settings:

1 Select System Preferences from the Apple menu.

2 Click Language & Text.

3 Click Language.

4 Make sure that the primary language you work in is at the top of the list. Drag other languages in the order you work in.

5 Click Formats.

6 Choose a Region to select how dates, times, numbers, currencies and measurements show up.

7 Close System Preferences by clicking the red button in the upper left corner of the window.

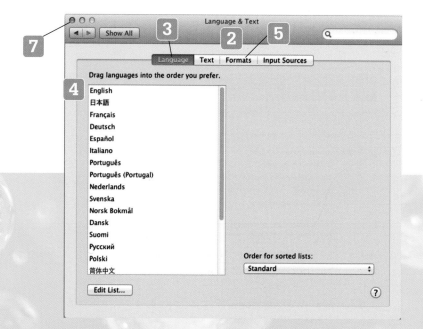

Setting up Bluetooth

If you have any Bluetooth-enabled devices, like iPhones, keyboards, mice or headsets, then you're probably wondering, 'Well, how do I make this stuff work with my Mac?'

It's pretty easy, really. All you need to do is enable Bluetooth on the device you want to pair up with your Mac, then tell your Mac about that device, then exchange tokens so that the two devices can communicate securely.

To set up Bluetooth:

1 Make sure that you've enabled Bluetooth on your device and placed it within range of your Mac (usually 3–5 feet).

2 Select System Preferences from the Apple menu.

3 Click Bluetooth.

4 If you haven't connected a device before, click Set Up New Device in the centre of the screen. Otherwise, click the + button in the first column to add a device.

5 Follow the wizard instructions to choose and pair up with the device.

6 At the end of the process, the wizard will give you a keyphrase that you need to enter into your device.

7 Once you enter the keyphrase in your device, it will connect with your Mac and you will see that device added to your list of Bluetooth devices.

8 Close System Preferences by clicking the red button in the upper left corner of the window.

WHAT DOES THIS MEAN?

Bluetooth: A wireless protocol for exchanging data over very short distances (usually measured in feet). It's what allows your headset to wirelessly connect to a mobile phone, or a digital camera to wirelessly transmit images to a photo printer.

Changing your display options

Some people are gifted with 20/20 vision (or better). Others have failing eyesight in their advanced decrepitude. But enough about me!

At some point, you'll want to adjust your display to accommodate your eyes. And once again, your Mac makes this really easy.

To change your display options:

1 Select System Preferences from the Apple menu.

2 Click Displays.

3 Click Display and choose a resolution from the list until your eyes tell you that things are 'all right'.

4 Adjust the brightness with the Brightness slider.

5 Make sure that you keep the box ticked next to Automatically adjust brightness as ambient light changes.

6 Close System Preferences by clicking the red button in the upper left corner of the window.

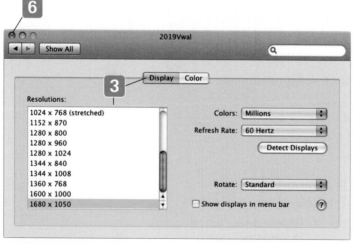

Making your Mac more energy efficient

In this day and age, who doesn't want to be more green and more friendly to Mother Earth? Well, Mac users have been eco-friendly for a long time, way longer than the latest eco-craze, and for good reason: if you're not working on something, then your Mac shouldn't be racking up a huge power bill.

To make your Mac more energy efficient:

1 Select System Preferences from the Apple menu.

2 Click Energy Saver.

3 Adjust how fast your Mac goes to sleep by adjusting the Computer sleep slider.

4 Adjust how fast your display goes to sleep by adjusting the Display sleep slider. A good place to start is 5 minutes.

5 Close System Preferences by clicking the red button in the upper left corner of the window.

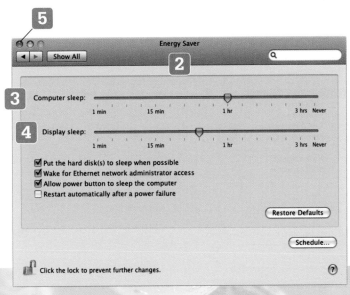

 ALERT: Remember that if you've set up a screen saver you might not see it at all if your machine is set to go to sleep!

Sharing a printer

If you've got more than one computer in the house or office but only one printer, you'll probably find yourself sharing a printer. After all, it's much cheaper than buying another printer!

To share a printer:

1 Select System Preferences from the Apple menu.

2 Click Sharing.

3 Tick the box next to Printer Sharing.

4 Tick the box next to the printer you want to share.

5 Close System Preferences by clicking the red button in the upper left corner of the window.

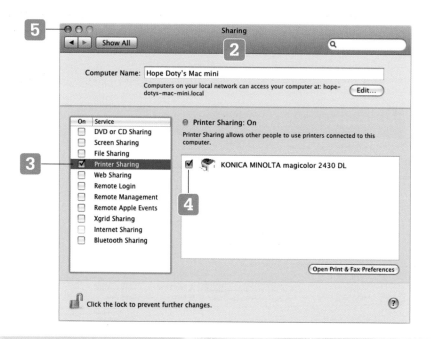

 **SEE ALSO:** If you're having trouble with your printer, check out the final section of this book – 'Top 10 Mac Problems Solved'.

Sharing files with another Mac

One day you'll find yourself needing to share your files with another Mac – it'll just make things easier than putting files on a thumb drive or emailing files back and forth. One of the things that Macs are really good at is seamless sharing of resources and that includes setting up secure areas that fellow Mac users can use to drop off (and pick up!) files.

To set up sharing of files on your Mac:

1 Select System Preferences from the Apple menu.

2 Click Sharing.

3 Tick the box next to File Sharing. This will automatically make the Public folder in your home area shared on the local network, creating a Dropbox folder within that folder that others can use to put files into.

4 Adjust the privileges that users have in the Public area. For example, you may only want to give others read privileges (they can only copy files from your Public area) or read and write privileges (they can copy files to and from the Public area).

5 Close System Preferences by clicking the red button in the upper left corner of the window.

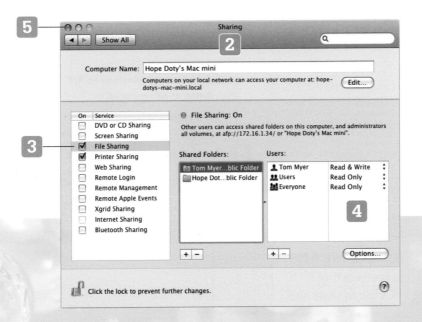

Sharing files with a PC

If you're working in an office with PCs and Macs, or a friend comes over to the house with a PC laptop, don't despair, sharing with a PC is pretty simple and straightforward. In fact, most of the instructions are the same as with a Mac, except you have to add a few more options.

To set up sharing of files on your Mac:

1 Select System Preferences from the Apple menu.

2 Click Sharing.

3 Tick the box next to File Sharing. This will automatically make the Public folder in your home area shared on the local network, creating a Dropbox folder within that folder that others can use to put files into.

4 Adjust the privileges that users have in the Public area. For example, you may only want to give others read privileges (they can only copy files from your Public area) or read and write privileges (they can copy files to and from the Public area).

5 Click Options.

6 Make sure that you tick the box next to Share files and folders using SMB.

7 Click Done.

8 Close System Preferences by clicking the red button in the upper left corner of the window.

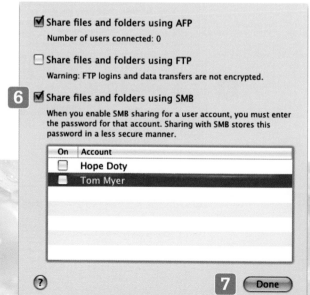

WHAT DOES THIS MEAN?

SMB: A file access protocol that Windows-based PCs use to share files on a network.

Setting up guest accounts

Your Mac is a powerful system capable of supporting the needs of multiple users. What this means is that you can have many guest accounts on the system, each of them with different privileges. For example, you might be the main user, but your kids or other house guests might need temporary access to the same machine.

Instead of giving them your own login credentials, it's much better to set up guest accounts for each person (or even a generic guest account in case someone comes over for dinner and needs to check their Gmail really quickly), because that way you can better control what's going on.

To set up a guest account:

1 Select System Preferences from the Apple menu.

2 Click Users & Groups.

3 To add an account, click the + button under Login Options. If this button is greyed out, you might need to unlock the screen. Click the lock symbol in the lower left and type in your administrative password.

4 Add details for the new account. You'll need to add a name, short name (or username), password and password hint. I would also suggest that you make this guest account a standard account, or if you're setting it up for a minor, a managed account with parental controls.

5 Click Create Account when you've finished.

6 If you had to unlock the screen to add the account, click the lock to relock the screen. This will keep others from making further changes.

7 Close System Preferences by clicking the red button in the upper left corner of the window.

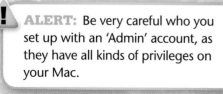

ALERT: Be very careful who you set up with an 'Admin' account, as they have all kinds of privileges on your Mac.

Setting date and time

It's highly unlikely that your Mac will ever get out of sync with the time server (and yes, there are servers on the Internet dedicated to keeping computers synched with the proper date and time), but just in case you need to, you can manually set date, time and time zone settings.

To set the date and time on your Mac:

1 Select System Preferences from the Apple menu.

2 Click Date & Time.

3 Click Date & Time in the top row of tabs.

4 If you want to set your date and time manually, make sure that you untick the Set date & time automatically tickbox. Once you do that, you can manually set a date with the calendar widget and a time with the clock widget.

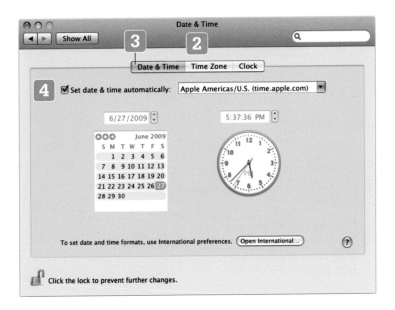

5 Click Time Zone in the top row of tabs.

6 Make sure that you've unticked the Set date & time automatically tickbox in the previous tab. Once you do that, you can manually set a time zone on the map.

7 Click Clock in the top row of tabs.

8 You can show the date and time in the Mac's menu bar by ticking the first tickbox.

9 You can make that clock appear digital or analogue by adjusting your View. You can make other changes as well, for example showing the day of the week or using a 24-hour clock by making the appropriate selections.

10 Close System Preferences by clicking the red button in the upper left corner of the window.

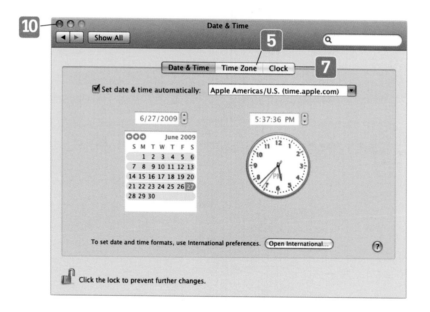

? DID YOU KNOW?

Your Mac will synch up with an NTP server (NTP stands for network time protocol) to keep the proper date and time based on your time zone. The automatic default is Apple's very own time server at time.apple.com.

Setting up speech recognition

If you've got certain motor disabilities (i.e. you tire easily from using a keyboard and mouse, or you're unable to use your arms and hands) and you would like to stay as independent as possible, then the Mac is your friend. It arrives with speech recognition built in – all you have to do is turn it on.

The speech recognition facilities can work with either an internal microphone or one you purchase. Speech recognition can listen for special keywords you say out loud that will tell it it's time to launch a command or application, or it can be set up to wait until you press a keyboard sequence. You can also set up custom commands that work with your set of applications.

To turn on speech recognition:

1 Select System Preferences from the Apple menu.

2 Click Speech.

3 Click Speech Recognition.

4 Make sure that you turn Speakable Items 'On' by clicking the appropriate radio button.

5 Click Settings to set up your microphone and special keywords.

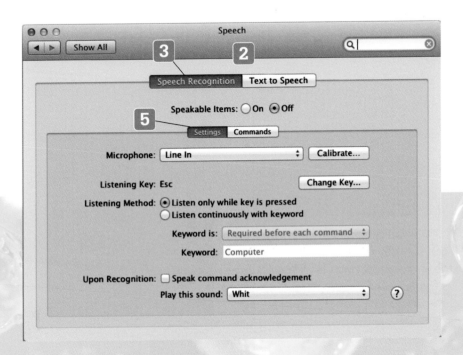

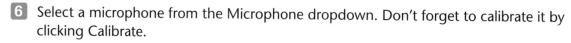

6 Select a microphone from the Microphone dropdown. Don't forget to calibrate it by clicking Calibrate.

7 Choose a listening method. You can set it to listen only when a certain key is pressed or to listen continuously.

8 If you choose to listen continuously, you might want to set up a keyword, like 'Computer', that will allow you to issue commands.

9 Close System Preferences by clicking the red button in the upper left corner of the window.

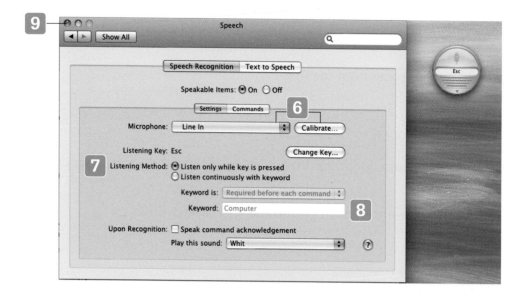

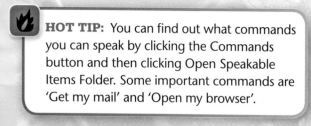

HOT TIP: You can find out what commands you can speak by clicking the Commands button and then clicking Open Speakable Items Folder. Some important commands are 'Get my mail' and 'Open my browser'.

Setting up keyboard shortcuts

Some people like to use their mouse to do stuff, while others like to use keyboard shortcuts. What's a keyboard shortcut? Well, it's exactly what it sounds like: a set of keys you press that gives you a shortcut to certain functionality.

For example, I've mentioned that you can start a search with Spotlight on the Mac by pressing ⌘ space on the keyboard. However, you may want some other key combination for that particular function because you can never remember it. Or you might want to add others.

1 Select System Preferences from the Apple menu.

2 Click Keyboard.

3 Click Keyboard Shortcuts.

4 Select an existing item from the list that you want to change.

5 Double-click the Shortcut portion until the background changes colour.

6 Press the key sequence you want to assign to the command, for example Shift ⌘ X.

7 Close System Preferences by clicking the red button in the upper left corner of the window.

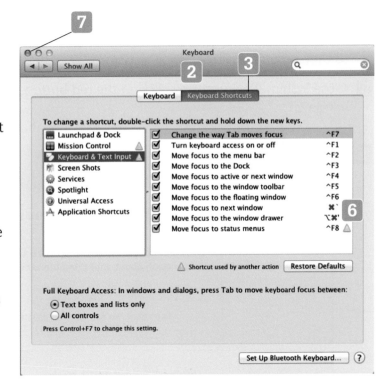

 HOT TIP: Windows users who migrate to Mac usually complain that pressing the Tab key doesn't allow them to move between certain form elements, like dropdowns. Well, here's the screen that will fix that problem. Just scroll down to the bottom and tick the radio button next to All controls under Full keyboard access.

Setting up software updates

It's a good idea to keep your Mac up to date. In fact, every once in a while the good people at Apple will offer patches, upgrades and other goodies that are ready to install via the Software Update system built into your Mac.

To manually change how often your Mac gets these updates, follow these steps:

1 Select System Preferences from the Apple menu.

2 Click Software Update.

3 Select a value from the Check for updates dropdown. A good place to start is weekly, as that way you won't be bugged all the time.

4 Do be sure to tick the box next to Download important updates automatically as this will install security patches, firmware updates and other critical updates as soon as they become available.

5 Close System Preferences by clicking the red button in the upper left corner of the window.

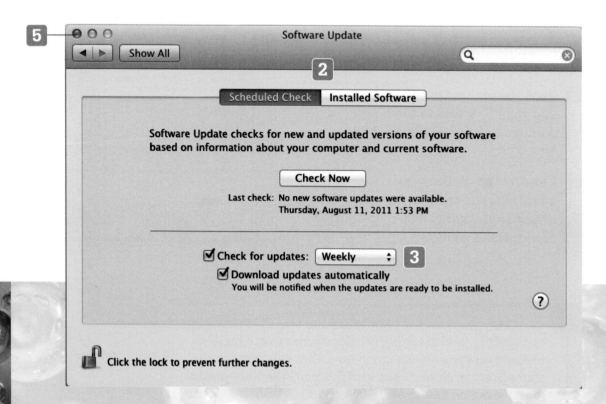

Top 10 Mac Problems Solved

Introduction

Just because you're on a Mac doesn't mean that you'll never have problems. It is a computer after all, and although it may be the most stable computer you'll ever use, it does come with its share of issues, problems and annoyances, no matter how small some of them are.

In this section I'm going to identify some of the annoyances that come up most often and show you how to get rid of them.

Problem 1: An application won't respond

Every once in a while, you'll notice that you'll be working on something and then the application you're working in will freeze up. You might see the so-called 'spinning beach ball of death' but won't be able to get back to what you were working on.

Hey – it happens, even on a Mac. You might have too many applications open at the same time, you might be crunching too much data for the amount of memory and CPU you have, or some other cause.

Here's how to unfreeze your application:

1 Control-click the application's icon in the Dock.

2 Choose Force Quit from the pop-up menu.

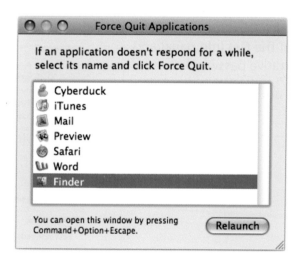

Problem 2: A folder won't open

If you double-click a folder and it won't open – or you can't seem to drag files into a particular folder – then you probably have a permissions problem.

Remember that underneath all the beauty of the Mac interface is a hard-core UNIX machine and that means that files and folders follow the rules of user permissions. It could be that the folder you're working on has had its permissions changed or altered by another person or process.

To find out for sure:

1 Control-click the folder in question and choose Get Info from the pop-up menu.

2 Scroll down to the Sharing & Permissions section. The user you're logged in as should have read and write privileges. If you don't, change those permissions.

3 You may need to unlock the panel to make this change. To do that, click the lock in the lower right-hand corner of the Get Info panel and enter your administrative password. Be sure to lock it back up after you've finished making changes.

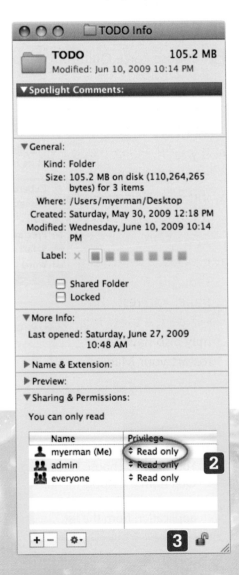

ALERT: You can only unlock a panel if you remember your administrative password. Keep it safe and secure, but memorable.

Problem 3: My wireless network has stopped working

Occasionally you'll be working happily and then find yourself unable to get on the Web or check email. If you're on a wireless connection, it could be any of a number of things:

- Check to make sure that your broadband router is still connected to the Internet. Check the router's user manual to figure out if there are any warning lights on the display that might indicate this.

- If it isn't connected to the Internet, the device may need to be restarted. If after a clean restart (usually by shutting off the power and rebooting, but check your router's user manual!) you still can't get on the Internet, your Internet service provider might be down. Please give them a call to find out.

- If the router is okay, make sure that any wireless access point on the router is working. You can do that easily enough by clicking the wireless icon on your Mac's menu bar and shutting off wireless, then turning it back on. When you turn wireless back on, you should see your wireless access point in the list.

- If you don't see it in the list, refer to your router's user manual to restart the wireless access point.

- If the wireless access point is working, use the Network Diagnostics tool in Safari to run through a series of tests. This diagnostic tool is easy to find as Safari will show you a blank page with a button that will run it if it can't get on the Internet.

- If all else fails, usually shutting down the router and restarting will do the trick. You may also have to restart your Mac.

Problem 4: My printer doesn't work

If you suddenly find yourself unable to print, you've got several ways to address the problem:

- Find out if the printer has power and is actually on.

- Check the printer to make sure that it isn't in diagnostic mode or has locked up in some way. You might need to restart your printer.

- Make sure that any network cables attaching the printer to the network are connected.

- If the printer is actually connected to another Mac on the network, make sure those cables are connected. Also, make sure that the Mac in question has Printer sharing turned on. (Open System Preferences, click Sharing, click Printer Sharing, select the printer from the list.)

- Make sure that you have current drivers for the printer. You can do this easily by removing the printer from your list of printers, then adding it again. (Click System Preferences, click Print & Fax, remove the current printer with the – button, add a new one with a + button, follow instructions.)

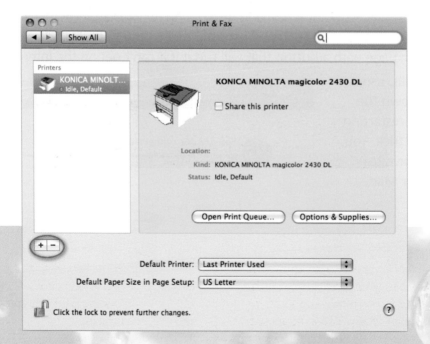

Problem 5: I can't empty the Trash

There are usually two reasons why the Trash won't empty: items in the Trash are owned by someone else or items in the Trash are locked.

- If you have locked items in the Trash, you can force-delete those items by holding down the command (⌘) key when you control-click the Trash icon and choosing Empty Trash from the pop-up menu.

- If you have items owned by someone else in the Trash, select those items in the Trash and control-click them. When the pop-up menu appears, choose Get Info, scroll down to Sharing & Permissions and make sure that your user has read and write permissions on the item.

- You can force the Trash to empty by doing this: press and hold the Option key, control-click the Trash, select Empty Trash from the pop-up menu, then release the Option key.

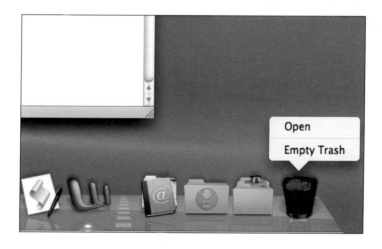

 HOT TIP: If you still can't empty the Trash, you may have a file in there that is being used by an open application. Simply quit the application in question (this may take some deduction on your part), then try to empty the Trash.

 HOT TIP: If quitting applications doesn't work, try logging back out and logging back in.

Problem 6: Documents open in the wrong application

If you double-click a text file and it opens in a graphics program (or vice versa) then you have some kind of mismatch going on between the type of file and the application it is associated with. To fix the problem:

1 Control-click the file in question, then choose Open With from the pop-up menu.

2 Instead of choosing the right application from the list (which will solve the problem only temporarily), click Other.

3 In the new screen, choose the application that should open this type of file, then tick the box next to 'Always Open With.'

4 Click Open.

Problem 7: The tab key doesn't work properly

If you're brand new to Macs then you've probably noticed something that you possibly liked about Windows that doesn't work now: you can't easily tab between all form elements when you're registering for something on the Web. If you encounter a dropdown, for example, the tab key won't work properly.

Well, here's how to fix that little problem:

1 Select System Preferences from the Apple menu.

2 Click Keyboard.

3 Click Keyboard Shortcuts.

4 Scroll down to the bottom of the screen and click the radio button next to All controls under Full keyboard access.

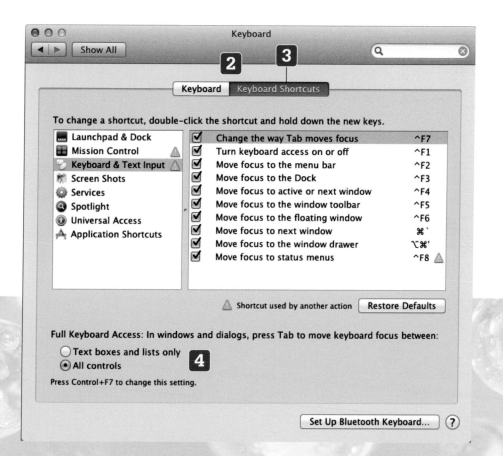

Problem 8: My Mac won't start!

If you turn on your Mac and see only a grey screen, then you just might have a little problem! It's okay, though, because there are different ways to get you back online.

You can do one of the following:

- Hold down the power button until the Mac turns back on. When it does power back on, hold down the Shift key. This will start the Mac in Safe Mode. You'll see a moving gear and the words 'Safe Boot' on the screen. Once the system runs a disk check and completes it, you can reboot the Mac.
- Reboot the machine and hold down ⌘ S while you reboot. This will open a command line mode, so don't panic! Type the following command: fsck –fy followed by the return key and let the program run – it should find any problems and fix them. Type reboot when the program has finished running.

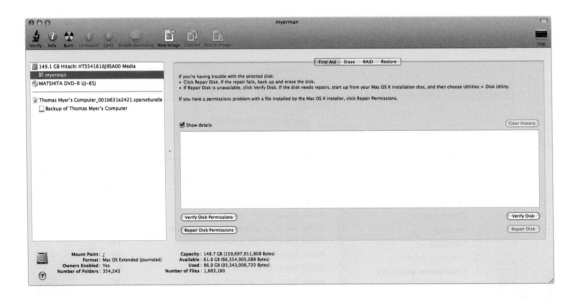

Problem 9: My Mac is completely frozen!

Another problem you might encounter occasionally is your Mac totally 100% freezing up on you. You'll know it because nothing you do will work – keyboard won't respond, mouse won't work at all and no amount of praying, crying, begging or screaming will make it come back. Even after that long coffee break you'll find that the machine is still frozen.

There's an easy fix for all this:

- Press the power button on your Mac until the screen goes blank and the Mac beeps. You can stop pressing the button now.
- When you see the Mac icon on a light grey background, you know you're okay. Next you'll see a light blue screen and then the Desktop.

? **DID YOU KNOW?**

The spinning beach ball is something you'll see occasionally if your Mac is working very hard to complete a task. In the image above, I opened several dozen applications before I saw the beach ball start spinning. Yes, your Mac is very robust!

Problem 10: I want to avoid data corruption and loss

Whether you're running a business or your life with your Mac, your data is invaluable. You've got music files, family photos, work documents, events, email, to-dos, movies, notes, spreadsheets and probably even a novel tucked away in different folders of your system. Losing any of that stuff would be a pain in the you-know-what.

Guess what? An ounce of prevention is worth a pound of cure, as my grandmother (and probably yours also!) used to say.

Here's how to make your life a lot less stressful:

- Don't just plug your Mac into any old wall outlet. Get a surge protector to protect yourself from power fluctuations, lightning strikes and other problems. Power fluctuations and outages are a good way to damage your hardware and corrupt files.

- Better yet, invest in a UPS (uninterruptible power supply). Each comes with a battery that feeds power to your system for 15–30 minutes during power outages (this should be enough time to get your systems turned off safely).

- Buy an external hard drive (200 GB should be more than enough) and attach it to your Mac with a FireWire cable. Then configure Time Machine to use that external hard drive as a backup. Turn it on and walk away – the first backup will take a few days, but after that, every hour Time Machine will do an incremental backup of your entire Mac. Whatever changes occur in that hour will be faithfully recorded and added to the backup. If you ever lose a file (or accidentally delete one), you can use Time Machine to restore it.

- Depending on the size of your external hard drive, Time Machine can keep bigger or smaller archives. I've found that a 500 GB drive can keep about three to four months worth of data. If you need more space, budget for a bigger backup solution.

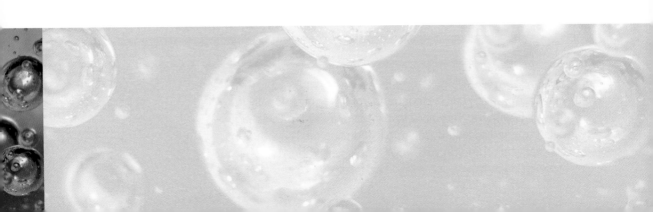

- If you have multiple Macs in the same small business or household, think about getting a Time Capsule instead. They come in 500 GB to 4 TB (terabyte) and can be attached to a wireless or wired network. Each Mac can then share the Time Capsule and use it for backups and restores.

Also available in the In Simple Steps series

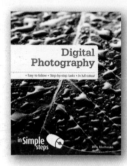

Digital Photography

9780273723516

Build your First Website

9780273745419

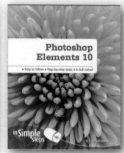

Photoshop Elements 10

9780273771296

Editing, Storing & Sharing Digital Photos

9780273744146

Windows 7

9780273729136

Web Design

9780273723530

Scanning and Restoring your Old Photos

9780273762591

Excel 2010

9780273736134

Researching your Family History Online

9780273761099

iPad

9780273744139

Using your Digital SLR Camera

9780273761105

Office 2010

9780273736127

in Simple steps